THE IMPORTANCE OF

Michelangelo

by
William W. Lace

Lucent Books, P.O. Box 289011, San Diego, CA 92198-9011

These and other titles are included in The Importance Of biography series:

Christopher Columbus	Chief Joseph
Marie Curie	Michelangelo
Walt Disney	Richard M. Nixon
Benjamin Franklin	Jackie Robinson
Galileo Galilei	Margaret Sanger
Thomas Jefferson	H.G. Wells

Library of Congress Cataloging-in-Publication Data

Lace, William W.
    Michelangelo / by William W. Lace
        p. cm. — (The Importance of)
    Includes bibliographical references and index.
    Summary: Describes the background and artistic career of the well-known Italian Renaissance painter, sculptor, and architect, Michelangelo Buonarroti.
    ISBN 1-56006-038-7 (alk. paper)
    1. Michelangelo Buonarroti, 1475-1564 —Juvenile literature.
2. Artists—Italy—Biography—Juvenile literature.
[1. Michelangelo Buonarroti, 1475-1564. 2. Artists.] I. Title.
II. Series.
N6923.B9L27   1993
709 .2 — dc20
[B]   92-46996
                                                              CIP
                                                               AC

Copyright 1993 by Lucent Books, Inc., P.O. Box 289011, San Diego, California, 92198-9011

LC 92-46996
ISBN 1-56006-038-7

Contents

Foreword

THE IMPORTANCE OF biography series deals with individuals who have made a unique contribution to history. The editors of the series have deliberately chosen to cast a wide net and include people from all fields of endeavor. Individuals from politics, music, art, literature, philosophy, science, sports, and religion are all represented. In addition, the editors did not restrict the series to individuals whose accomplishments have helped change the course of history. Of necessity, this criterion would have eliminated many whose contribution was great, though limited. Charles Darwin, for example, was responsible for radically altering the scientific view of the natural history of the world. His achievements continue to impact the study of science today. Others, such as Chief Joseph of the Nez Percé, played a pivotal role in the history of their own people. While Joseph's influence does not extend much beyond the Nez Percé, his nonviolent resistance to white expansion and his continuing role in protecting his tribe and his homeland remain an inspiration to all.

These biographies are more than factual chronicles. Each volume attempts to emphasize an individual's contributions both in his or her own time and for posterity. For example, the voyages of Christopher Columbus opened the way to European colonization of the New World. Unquestionably, his encounter with the New World brought monumental changes to both Europe and the Americas in his day. Today, however, the broader impact of Columbus's voyages is being critically scrutinized. *Christopher Columbus,* as well as every biography in The Importance Of series, includes and evaluates the most recent scholarship available on each subject.

Each author includes a wide variety of primary and secondary source quotations to document and substantiate his or her work. All quotes are footnoted to show readers exactly how and where biographers derive their information, as well as provide stepping stones to further research. These quotations enliven the text by giving readers eyewitness views of the life and times of each individual covered in The Importance Of series.

Finally, each volume is enhanced by photographs, bibliographies, chronologies, and comprehensive indexes. For both the casual reader and the student engaged in research, The Importance Of biographies will be a fascinating adventure into the lives of people who have helped shape humanity's past, present, and will continue to shape its future.

Important Dates in the Life of Michelangelo

Michelangelo is born in Caprese, Italy, where his father is mayor; Sent to live at Settignano after his father is recalled to Florence.

1475

Apprenticed to Domenico Ghirlandaio in Florence.

1488

Returns to Medici palace, later flees to Venice and Bologna; leaves Florence again when Piero de' Medici and family are deposed.

1489

Leaves Ghirlandaio to study with Bertol-do in Medici sculpture garden.

1490

Goes to live in Medici palace.

1492

Death of Lorenzo de' Medici.

1494

Carves *Bacchus.*

Carves *Pietà;* Savonarola is burned at the stake.

1496

**1497-
1499**

Returns from Rome to Florence; sculpts *David* in Florence.

Commissioned to paint *Battle of Cascina* on wall of council hall in Florence's Palazzo Vecchio; begins work on *Madonna Pitti, Madonna Taddei, Tondo Doni,* and cartoons for *Battle of Cascina;* summoned to Rome by Julius II; assigned to carve Julius's tomb; flees to Florence but returns to Bologna after being forgiven by Julius.

**1501-
1504**

Works on bronze of Julius in Bologna; begins work on Sistine Chapel ceiling.

**1504-
1506**

1508

Death of Julius II; Leo X (Giovanni de' Medici) becomes pope.

Sistine Chapel ceiling is finished.

1512

1513

Summoned to Rome by Leo X; ordered to construct San Lorenzo façade in Florence.

Death of Donato Bramante.

1514

Death of Leonardo da Vinci.

1516

1519

San Lorenzo façade canceled; death of Raphael; Cardinal Giulio de' Medici commissions Medici tomb in San Lorenzo.

Clement VII (Giulio de' Medici) is elected pope, and orders work on Medici tomb resumed.

1520

1523

Michelangelo is named governor of fortifications of Florence; flees from Florence to Venice.

1527

Sack of Rome by troops of Emperor Charles V; Medici family evicted from Florence.

1529

1530

Returns to Florence under safe conduct; continues work on fortifications; works on Medici tomb; Florence falls; Michelangelo is pardoned by Clement VII and continues work on Medici tomb.

Returns to Rome wanting to resume work on Julius's tomb; moves between Rome and Florence; leaves Florence, never to return; arrives in Rome two days before death of Clement VII.

**1532-
1534**

**1534-
1541**

The Conversion of St. Paul and *The Crucifixion of St. Peter* are painted in the Pauline Chapel of the Vatican.

**1541-
1550**

Paints *The Last Judgment;* meets Vittoria Colonna.

**1547-
1564**

Death of Vittoria Colonna; Michelangelo is named architect of Saint Peter's; carves *The Deposition of Christ;* works on Saint Peter's in Rome.

Michelangelo dies in his house in Rome.

1564

A Lasting Imprint

Greatness may be measured by what a person accomplishes during his or her lifetime, and importance by what a person causes to be done or accomplished by others. A surgeon may be great in skill or technique but is important only if his or her work leads to advances in surgery. A philosopher may think great thoughts, but they are not important unless they are spread to others. People are considered important in history only if they leave a lasting imprint upon the world through their works or deeds.

Michelangelo Buonarroti was such a person. The paintings, statues, and buildings created by this homely, reclusive, often abrasive artist are among the most beautiful ever known. He and his works are important, however, because they represent a break with the past and a signpost to the future.

Genius is one of the most overused words in the English language, yet it best describes Michelangelo. There is no clue as to where his immense talent came from. There was no history of artistic ability or even appreciation of art in his family. He had little formal training, and his teachers—even the old masters whose works he studied—had no dominant influence. The inspiration for the bold, new directions Michelangelo followed in art and architecture seemed to come from within. The artists of his time could say only that Michelangelo was a gift from God.

Nothing like Michelangelo's art had ever been seen before. The Renaissance was the period in European history that began about 1300 and lasted until the seventeenth century during which art, literature, and science flourished. The Renaissance brought a new realism to art, freeing it from the stiff formality of the preceding centuries. For Michelangelo, however, portraying something as it appeared in nature was not enough. He wanted to express emotions and feelings through physical forms. Gradually, over his long career, his works became less realistic. Michelangelo's goal was to portray ideas rather than people, something not even the ancient Greeks and Romans, to whom Renaissance artists turned for inspiration, had done.

Michelangelo's art had a direct influence on that of others. Artists from all over Europe traveled to Italy to study and copy his works. His innovations in architecture have been imitated through the years and are found in many public buildings today. His techniques, especially in the drawing of the human body, have been used by painters from his day to ours. Many of those who tried to copy

Michelangelo, unfortunately, could capture only the outward appearance of his works, not the spirit behind them.

Michelangelo's boldness and his willingness to break the established rules were perhaps more important than the works themselves. By discovering new methods of expression, by finding new directions, he encouraged other artists through his example to do the same. Painters and sculptors no longer felt bound to the past and were free to experiment. Modern, abstract art can even be traced back to Michelangelo because these artists, too, search for the new and different.

The Role of the Artist

Michelangelo was important not only for influencing artists but also for causing the public to reevaluate its view of artists. Before his time, the best artists might have the respect of those for whom they worked, but it was the same respect that might be given to an especially talented tailor or a competent carpenter. Artists were considered craftsmen. Michelangelo's fame, however, was greater than that of any artist before him. He was honored and respected. Kings, dukes, and popes vied with one another for his services and treated him almost as an equal. His irritability, his temper, and his tendency to leave work unfinished were forgiven because of his genius. Michelangelo was the person most responsible for the idea that

A bust of the artistic genius of the Renaissance, Michelangelo.

great artists are somehow superhuman and should not be judged by ordinary standards.

It was fortunate for Michelangelo, and for the world, that he lived when he did. The civilization of Europe, which would be carried throughout the world in the next centuries, was changing. Society was open to new ideas. The art world had broken free from hundreds of years of little change. It was ready for a giant, a larger-than-life figure who would give it a new direction for the future. Michelangelo was this giant.

Chapter 1

An Early Talent

Michelangelo's father, Ludovico di Buonarroti Simoni, was a proud man. He was not a rich man, just a proud one.

From the mid-1200s to the mid-1400s, the Buonarroti Simoni family had been important in the northern Italian city of Florence. They were prosperous traders and money changers. They frequently held positions on the governing councils of the city. Ludovico claimed that the family was descended from royalty, although this has never been proved.

From about 1450, however, the family's fortunes declined. Ludovico's grandfather had lost most of the family's wealth. Ludovico and his brother, Francesco, inherited only a small farm in the hills near Florence by the village of Settignano and a disputed title to a house in the city.

The two brothers and their families lived in a house rented from Ludovico's brother-in-law. It was in the Via dei Bentaccordi, a small, crooked street near the church of Santa Croce close to the Arno

The city of Florence as it looked in the fifteenth century when Michelangelo was born.

River. The area had once been a part of Florence where rich families lived, but now it was occupied mostly by small merchants and craftsmen. Here, the Buonarroti families lived on the income from the farm. They were poor but respectable.

Family pride was important to Ludovico, perhaps because it was almost all he had. He would rather remain poor than learn a trade. To work with his hands, he thought, would bring disgrace on the family name.

So, it was not until Ludovico was thirty, in the year 1475, that he obtained his first paying job—the minor government post of *podesta*, or mayor, of Caprese, a village in the mountainous area governed by Florence some forty miles southeast of the city. Here, he took his pregnant, nineteen-year-old wife, Francesca, and their infant son Leonardo to live in a partially ruined castle. The Arno River lay a few miles to the west, running toward Florence and then to the sea. Closer, to the east, a swift mountain stream, the Singerna, rushed south to join the Tiber, which flowed on to Rome.

It was here that Michelangelo, named in honor of the archangel Michael, was born early on the morning of Monday, March 6, 1475. It was fitting that he was born between Florence and Rome, since both were to play such important roles in his life and career. One writer said Michelangelo was "destined to spend his life in these two cities, passing like a vagrant force of nature from one to the other, so that his talents enriched both and helped inspire each in turn to a profuse artistic flowering unmatched since."[1]

Gift from God

No one in Michelangelo's family had ever exhibited any artistic ability. His early biographers thought his talent was a gift from God. In this poem, written about 1535 and taken from Michelangelo: A Self-Portrait, *Michelangelo agreed with them.*

"If my rude hammer the unwilling stone
To human form and attitude doth mold,
It moves with him, who doth it guide and hold,
His will and impulse taking for its own.
But one diviner doth in heaven abide,
Which shapeth beauty with no hand to aid;
No hammer is, save by another, made,
Then doth th' eternal one make all beside.
And as the hammer that is raised on high,
With greater force doth on the forge descend,
So that, to mold my own, to heaven is gone.
Whence mine unperfected must useless lie,
Unless that instrument divine shall lend
Its aid in heaven, which here availed alone."

An Unartistic Family

It is hard to see from where Michelangelo's talents came. No one in the Buonarroti family had ever been an artist. In a time and place famous for its art, there is no record of any of his relatives ever buying a painting or statue. Ascanio Condivi, who knew Michelangelo well and was one of his early biographers, attempted to explain his genius through the "science" of astrology. Astrologers claimed that the position of the stars and planets in the sky at the time of a person's birth influenced the future and even determined that person's abilities. Condivi wrote:

> A fine birth, certainly, and one which showed already how great the boy was to be and how great his genius; because the fact of having received Mercury and Venus in the second house [part of the sky], the house ruled by Jupiter, and with benign aspect, promised what later followed: that such a birth must be of a noble and lofty genius, destined to succeed universally in any undertaking, but principally in those arts which delight the senses, such as painting, sculpture, and architecture.[2]

Giorgio Vasari, Michelangelo's friend, pupil, and biographer, did not rely on the heavens but said instead that Michelangelo was a gift from God to the world.

> While industrious and choice spirits . . . endeavoured to attain to the height of knowledge by imitating the greatness of Nature in all things, the great Ruler of Heaven looked down and, seeing these vain and fruitless efforts and the presumptuous opinion of man more removed from truth than light from darkness, resolved, in order to rid him of these errors, to send to earth a genius universal in each art, to show single-handed the perfection of line and shadow, and who should give relief to his paintings, show a sound judgment in sculpture, and in architecture should render habitations convenient, safe, healthy, pleasant, well-proportioned, and enriched with various ornaments. He further endowed him with true moral philosophy and a sweet poetic spirit, so that the world should marvel at the singular eminence of his life and works and all his actions, seeming rather divine than earthly.[3]

Michelangelo Leaves His Family

Less than a month passed after Michelangelo's birth before Ludovico's term as *podesta* was over. The family moved back to Florence to the house in the Via dei Bentaccordi. This, however, was not to be Michelangelo's real home. Soon, Francesca was expecting a third child. She was a frail woman, and she found pregnancy and the care of two infant sons to be too much. Michelangelo, still less than six months old, was sent to live with a woman in Settignano near the Buonarroti farm who was paid to nurse and care for him.

Michelangelo's nurse was the wife of a stonecutter and the daughter of another. The stonecutters took the *duro sasso*, or rough stone boulders, from the many quarries in the area to their cottage and

With mallet and chisel, a stonecutter plies his trade.
Michelangelo's first years were spent in the home of a
stonecutter.

there used mallets, chisels, and saws to
shape the stone into blocks for later use in
buildings. Certainly, Michelangelo could
hear from his cradle the sounds made by
these tools. He probably later played
among the blocks and had mallets and
chisels as his first toys. Late in life, he jok-
ingly told his friend Vasari, "What good I
have comes from the pure air of your native Arezzo [Settignano was in the area of
Arezzo], and also because I sucked in chisels and hammers with my nurse's milk."[4]

Every so often, Michelangelo returned
to his parents' house. The time he spent
there was probably not pleasant compared
to life among the stonecutters. Ludovico,
moody over the family's poverty, had little
time for the boy. Francesca, busier and

more frail than ever after the birth of her
third son, could pay little attention to her
second. Eventually, there would be fourth
and fifth sons before the exhausted
Francesca died when Michelangelo was six
years old.

After his mother's death, Michelangelo lived for four years with the stonecutters at Settignano. He visited his father
and four brothers only rarely. A drawing,
said to be by Michelangelo, can still be
seen on the wall of the house at Settignano. He probably learned the basics of
carving marble at this time, but no one
knows for certain.

First School

In 1485, Ludovico remarried. Ten-year-old
Michelangelo was brought back to Florence, unable to read or write, speaking
with the accent of a peasant. His clothes
were covered with the marble dust of Settignano. His father put him in schoolmas-
ter Francesco da Urbino's local school,
and although Condivi said Michelangelo
had reached the "right age," most boys of
good family in Florence began lessons at
the age of six.

One biographer, Howard Hibbard,
upon considering Michelangelo's poetry,
claimed he must have begun school earlier. "All of this [the poetry] is conceivable
without much formal schooling," he
wrote, "but he must have had more than
we know about."[5]

Michelangelo was not a bad student.
He was not a good student, either. The
trouble was that he cared only for art,
something his family could not understand. Whenever he could steal away, he

mingled with artists and their apprentices in studios around the city. He spent most of his time drawing, whether in school or out. Vasari wrote that because of this, "his father and seniors scolded and sometimes beat him, thinking that such things were base and unworthy of their noble house."[6]

One apprentice, Francesco Granacci, was his closest friend even though Granacci was six years older. Although Granacci possessed only modest talent, he recog-nized Michelangelo's gifts and urged him to abandon school and become an artist.

Ludovico did not agree. He saw no dif-ference between the artist who carved stat-ues and the laborer who carved building blocks. He was determined to see Michelangelo become a merchant. Lu-dovico thought it undignified for his son to make a living working with his hands.

Condivi said that Michelangelo was "resented and quite often beaten unrea-

The Pull of Art

When Michelangelo was ten years old, his father placed him in the school of Francesco da Urbino. In his biography The Life of Michelange-lo, *Ascanio Condivi relates how the young man later neglected school in favor of art.*

"Although he profited somewhat from the study of let-ters, at the same time nature and the heavens, which are difficult to withstand, were drawing him toward painting; so that he could not resist running off here and there to draw whenever he could steal some time and seeking the company of painters. Of these, he was very close to one Francesco Granacci, a pupil of Domenico del Ghirlandaio, who perceived the boy's inclination and burning desire and resolved to help him, and he urged him on continually in his undertaking, now providing him with drawings, now taking him along to his master's workshop or wherever there might be some work of art from which he could benefit. His effect was so strong, combined as it was with nature's constant stimulus, that Michelangelo completely abandoned the study of letters. On this account he was resented and quite often beaten unreasonably by his father and his father's brothers who, being impervious to the excellence and nobility of art, despised it and felt that its appearance in their family was a disgrace. Despite the very great distress this caused Michelangelo, it was nevertheless not enough to turn him back; instead, he was emboldened and wanted to at-tempt the use of color."

sonably by his father and his father's brothers who, being impervious to the excellence and nobility of art, detested it and felt that its appearance in their family was a disgrace."[7] This had no effect on Michelangelo. He loved his family, and throughout his long life, he was a dutiful son and brother. But where his art was concerned, there was no compromise. Ludovico, for all the ragings and the beatings, was no match for a stubborness that would later confound popes and princes. Biographer Charles de Tolnay said that Michelangelo "felt very early the spiritual narrowness of his family world, from which he turned away at an early age."[8]

Entering the World of Art

Finally, when Michelangelo was thirteen, his father decided to make the best of the situation. On April 1, 1488, he took his rebellious son to the *bottega*, or studio, of Domenico Ghirlandaio, where Granacci was an apprentice. Perhaps Ghirlandaio

knew of the young man from Granacci and recognized his talent. Perhaps Ludovico was a shrewd bargainer. Whatever the reason, Michelangelo was to earn a salary

Florentine artist Domenico Ghirlandaio was Michelangelo's first art teacher.

Fatherly Concern

Michelangelo's father, Ludovico Buonarroti, never understood his son or his son's work, but he always had plenty of advice. This letter, written to Michelangelo in Rome about 1500 and taken from Michelangelo: A Self-Portrait, *showed Ludovico's practical nature.*

"Buonarroto [Michelangelo's brother] tells me that you live at Rome with great economy, or rather penuriousness [spending as little as possible]. Now economy is good, but penuriousness is evil, seeing that it is a vice displeasing to God and men, and moreover injurious both to soul and body. So long as you are young, you will be able for a time to endure these hardships; but when the vigor of youth fails, then diseases and infirmities make their appearance; for these are caused by personal discomforts, mean living, and penurious habits. As I said, economy is good; but, above all things, shun stinginess. Live discreetly well, and see you have what is needful. Whatever happens, do not expose yourself to physical hardships; for in your profession, if you were once to fall ill (which God forbid), you would be a ruined man. Above all things, take care of your head, and keep it moderately warm, and see that you never wash; have yourself rubbed down, but do not wash."

instead of Ludovico having to pay the master painter to teach his son. When Ludovico returned from his errand, he wrote in his journal:

> Know this . . . 1st April that I, Ludovico di Lionardo Buonarroti apprentice my son Michelangelo to Domenico and David di Tommaso di Currado [Domenico and his brother David] for the next three years, with the following agreements: that the said Michelangelo shall remain with them that time to learn to paint and practice that art and shall do what they bid him, and they shall give him 24 florins in the three years, 6 in the first, 8 in the second and 10 in the third, in all 96 lire.

Below is written,

> Michelangelo has received 2 gold florins this 16th April, and I, Ludovico di Lionardo, his father have received 12 lire 12 soldi.[9]

Michelangelo entered the world of art.

2 Entering the World of Art

Michelangelo's genius could not have found a more hospitable environment than Florence in the year 1488. The world had been changing dramatically for almost two hundred years. That change, which began first in literature, later in art, and still later in science, was reaching its height when Michelangelo entered Ghirlandaio's *bottega*.

Interest in culture, learning, and art had been renewed. Vasari, who recorded the lives of hundreds of artists in addition to Michelangelo's, called it a *renascita*, a rebirth. French writers later translated this into *renaissance*, the term we use today. The change was not in art only but, as historian Wallace Ferguson wrote, was "a general awakening or rebirth of human intellect and personality, the beginning of the modern world."[10]

Art patrons gather in the courtyard of a Florence museum. The medieval rebirth, or renaissance, of art and culture began in Italy.

The Renaissance replaced the Middle Ages, the period of seven hundred years or so between the fall of the Roman Empire and about 1300. During the Middle Ages, people followed two primary sources of authority, the nobility and the Roman Catholic church. By 1300, much of this authority had been lost. Many nobles had been killed by almost constant warfare, and their wealth decreased as a rich merchant class grew in the cities. The church had declined in power, too. It became a political force as much as a spiritual one and took sides with kings and waged wars. The popes and their cardinals and bishops often cared more for wealth than for religion. Many people no longer believed that these men were the spokesmen of God.

With the two principal sources of authority in decline, people began to look elsewhere for guidance. In Italy around 1300, scholars began to look to ancient Rome. Historian John R. Hale wrote:

> To go forward it was necessary to go back; to advance from the Middle Ages it was necessary to return to antiquity and relearn the lessons which had enabled Rome to produce her great civilization. . . . Men sensed that things were not going as they should— in either church or state—and longed for some sort of regeneration, some sort of revival. Rome, once the secular [nonreligious] as well as the spiritual capital of the world, became the focus of these aspirations. Men yearned for the rebirth, the renaissance, of Rome's past glories.[11]

It was no accident that the Renaissance began in Italy. Politically, Italy was a patchwork of independent kingdoms, dukedoms, and city-states. Geographically,

A wealthy fifteenth-century Italian merchant inspects a shipment of goods at the docks.

Italy was at the center of trade. Goods and wealth flowed from Africa and the Middle East into Italy and from there to the rest of Europe. Italian banks were the center of finance.

This trade through Italy created a wealthy merchant class, one that was largely independent because of the lack of a strong, central government, such as that in France or England. These merchants saw themselves as descendants, both literally and in spirit, of the Romans. Bankers, lawyers, and merchants began to study Roman legal codes. They read, for pleasure, the writings of Cicero, Ovid, Homer, Plato, and other Greek and Roman philosophers, historians, and poets. They thought that by studying ancient writers, they could learn how to re-create the days when the world was ruled from Italy.

A Time of Great Change

The people of the Renaissance knew they were living in a time of great change. They thought they had rediscovered, after centuries of ignorance, the knowledge of Greece and Rome. They saw the Renaissance as a sudden beam of light illuminating what had been darkness. In the mid-1400s, poet Matteo Palmieri wrote that everyone should "thank God that it has been permitted to him to be born in this new age, so full of hope and promise, which already rejoices in a greater array of nobly-gifted souls than the world has seen in the thousand years that have preceded it."[12]

Studying the ancient authors had a great impact on the writers of the early Renaissance, such as Dante, Boccaccio, and Petrarch. These men were very different from the writers of the Middle Ages, most of whom were monks or priests who wrote on religious topics. People of the Renaissance wrote more about everyday matters—love, money, wars, commerce, and law.

In fact, everyday life took on a whole

An Intellectual Revolution

In his book Meaning of the Renaissance and Reformation, *Richard L. DeMolen describes how the Renaissance upset the established order of the Middle Ages and caused people to wonder about their place in God's universe.*

"The age of Renaissance and Reformation may be characterized as an intellectual revolution of immeasurable internal and external dimensions—a movement which was evolutionary in its origins but revolutionary in its effects. The revolution was so shattering that it transformed the neatly labeled microcosm [little world] that was medieval Europe into the dynamic and divergent macrocosm [expanded world] of the Renaissance. . . . Man realized in this period that his perception of the world was no longer valid and had to change, and that with his changing perception the world changed. Where once man had been positioned securely at the center of the universe, in a hierarchical [fixed] order, there were now limitless horizons. Man was confronted by no known boundaries, no permanent definitions, no certain knowledge. Man was at a loss for where he was and had to make a new place for himself."

new importance. In the Middle Ages, people had been more concerned about preparing for heaven than with their existence on earth. Everything that they accomplished was supposed to be for the glory of God, so education focused on the study of religion. In the Renaissance, the rise in commerce and the renewed interest in Greece and Rome allowed people to study such subjects as economics, history, and law in addition to religion.

The Birth of Humanism

Historian Richard DeMolen wrote that during the Renaissance, "man's mind was freed . . . it was stretched, enriched, and deepened."[13] The condition and problems of humankind began to be studied. A Renaissance scholar, Leonardo Bruni, called these studies *humanitas*, from which we get our term *humanism*. The Renaissance brought about a belief that people, through their individual works, could improve the world. Philosopher Gianozzo Manetti wrote in 1452:

> For everything that surrounds us is our work, the work of man; all dwellings, all castles, all cities, all the edifices throughout the whole world, which are so numerous and of such quality that they resemble the works of angels rather than men. Ours are the paintings, the sculptures; ours are the trades, sciences and philosophical systems. Ours are all inventions and all kinds of languages and literary works, and when we think about their necessary employment [how they are used], we are compelled so much more to admiration and astonishment.[14]

Art

The revival of classical culture and the new emphasis on humanism had a profound impact on art as well. Roman statues—dug out of the ground, cleaned, and polished—became prized possessions in the homes of the wealthy.

These artworks were far different from those of the Middle Ages, most of which had a flat, lifeless, unreal appearance. Artists during the Middle Ages portrayed people who showed little or no expression or emotion. It was difficult to tell if objects

Religious themes were the chief subject of medieval artists. This madonna and Christ child was painted by thirteenth-century Italian master Cimabue.

in paintings were supposed to be near or far away and their sizes, in relationship to one another, were confusing. The classical works, however, had a natural appearance that had not been seen for hundreds of years.

Renaissance artists, like writers, were inspired by the works of Greece and Rome and studied them in order to make their own works more lifelike. They also studied nature itself, trying to portray people and things the way they appeared to the human eye instead of imitating the flat formality of the medieval painters.

Four men—painters Giotto and Masaccio, sculptor Donatello, and architect Brunelleschi—led the way in this artistic revolution. They, perhaps more than any others, had a profound influence on Michelangelo and other Renaissance artists.

Giotto

Giotto, who lived from 1266 to 1337, was the earliest. He is considered the dividing point between the art of the Middle Ages and that of the Renaissance. He was the first to attempt to achieve perspective, or visual reality—to paint buildings, rooms, people, and objects in correct proportion to one another. By doing so, he created a feeling of depth unknown in paintings of the Middle Ages.

Just as important as visual reality was the emotional reality Giotto brought to painting. Instead of standing in stiff poses, facing the viewer, his people look real. Their natural poses and the way they react with one another convey real emotions.

Giotto revolutionized art. According to the *Encyclopedia of Painting*:

Giotto's painting The Visitation *has the three-dimensional perspective and natural poses typical of Renaissance painting.*

With him, and his generation, the practice of imitating the formulas and conventions of other artists was replaced or at least supplemented by the study of nature in the form of models and actual landscape. The effect of these innovations was profound and instantaneous. Within a generation the Italian Romanesque and Byzantine styles [the styles of the Middle Ages] were wiped out. . . . Giotto's art is a visual expression of the humanization and secularization [having to do with nonreligious matters] of thought and life that announced the Renaissance in Europe.[15]

After Giotto, little progress was made

toward realism during the rest of the 1300s, and artists seemed contented to copy his style. As Leonardo da Vinci, who was to be Michelangelo's greatest artistic rival, wrote:

> Afterwards [after Giotto] this art declined again, because everyone imitated the pictures that were already done . . . until Masaccio showed by his perfect works how those who take for their standard anyone but nature—the mistress of all masters—weary themselves in vain.[16]

Masaccio

Masaccio lived from 1401 to 1428. He was one of the first painters to study ancient Greek and Roman works. Perhaps this is why his people look even more real than those of Giotto. In Masaccio's work, the clothing is drawn in such a way that the viewer can tell there are muscles and bones underneath. Masaccio was the first artist since ancient times to try to show realistic human anatomy.

Early Renaissance master Masaccio was the first artist to depict the human figure realistically rather than in the stylized, two-dimensional way of medieval artists.

Toward Realism in Art

In his book Renaissance, *John R. Hale describes how the development of a class of wealthy businessmen in Florence during the Renaissance affected the art that was produced in the city.*

"The taste of the rich, then, set the tone for art. But the mercantile [business] atmosphere of Florence as a whole may also have provided encouragement. Art follows its own inner laws of growth and the special talents of individual artists, but it can also be affected by the tempo of a society. Working in the midst of financial realists, the Florentine artist may have been stimulated to move toward realism faster than he would have elsewhere. The average Florentine businessman knew what things were for and what they cost—houses, fields, vineyards. The thought of profit was close to the surface of his mind. This consciousness of real value, as opposed to symbolic value, carried over into other areas of his life. He was aware of his own worth as a person. Other men might do great deeds on the battlefield for which they would be remembered by poets and chroniclers, but he, too, was a man of accomplishments: he had made money, paid his taxes, kept careful accounts. He wanted to be remembered by posterity. So he had himself painted into the pictures he ordered for his church—a supplicant kneeling in a corner, a bystander in a crowd. And since there is no point in being painted unless you can be recognized, he asked to be painted as he was: it is no coincidence that Florence was first to stress realistic portraiture. These merchantlike qualities did not actually bring about Giotto's unique way of recording the world, or the style of Masaccio, but they almost certainly sustained them and helped them to have followers."

Masaccio also improved on Giotto's technique of perspective. His most important contribution, however, was to make paintings appear more real by using light and shadow to make figures look rounder and more firm. In his paintings, for the first time, there is a single source of light.

To the viewer, it is as if the sun or a window or a candle is shining on the scene from one side. This light source may be out of sight, but it casts shadows on the objects in the painting. This use of light and shadows is called *chiaroscuro*, a term formed from the Italian words for "light" and "dark."

Donatello

Donatello combined this new realism and the enthusiasm for ancient art and applied them to sculpture. The saints as portrayed during the Middle Ages were just as stiff in statues as they were in paintings. Most were made to be placed in narrow spaces and to be seen only from the front. Donatello re-created the three-dimensional sculpture of Greece and Rome and added to it a new understanding of human anatomy—how the human form is shaped by the muscles underneath the skin. His statue of Saint George is so lifelike that Michelangelo, when he first saw it, is supposed to have commanded, "March!"

Throughout his long career (he lived from 1386 to 1466), Donatello continued to be influenced by Greek and Roman art. He applied a classical style to biblical themes. This is best seen in his bronze *David*, the first life-size nude figure made since ancient Rome.

Brunelleschi

Brunelleschi lived from 1377 to 1446, and he shared Donatello's enthusiasm for Roman art. There is even the possibility that they traveled to Rome together shortly after 1400. Brunelleschi was an architect, and in studying the ancient buildings, he made an important discovery. He realized that perspective could be explained in mathematical terms. He found that by applying formulas, he could always draw ob-

Inspired by ancient Greek and Roman sculpture, Saint George *(left) by Donatello and the seated figure by Brunelleschi (right) look like real people.*

jects in their correct proportions. Depth could be achieved by making the lines in a drawing or painting seem to come together at a single point.

Brunelleschi's buildings, based on those of Rome but with a style all his own, would greatly influence later architects, including Michelangelo. His dome of the great cathedral in Florence, known as the Duomo, served as Michelangelo's model for the dome of Saint Peter's in Rome. In fact, when asked if he could build a dome for Saint Peter's bigger than Brunelleschi's in Florence, he replied, "Bigger, yes, but not more beautiful."[17]

Florence—Center of the Arts

In addition to being the creators of the Renaissance style of art and influencing Michelangelo and others, Giotto, Masac-cio, Donatello, and Brunelleschi had one other thing in common. They all were born in Florence or did most of their work there. Florence was the cultural center of Italy. John R. Hale wrote:

> Florence not only produced a series of great men; it supported an atmosphere of inquiry and experiment that made it a great laboratory. It was the testing ground for most of the Renaissance's political and artistic ideas. From the early fourteenth to the mid-sixteenth century no other city in Italy, indeed in Europe, kept up such a steady pressure of intellectual attainment.[18]

Certainly, as a center of banking and the wool business, Florence was a wealthy city. Its citizens were well-off and, for the time, well educated. It was said that even workmen in the streets could recite portions of the *Divine Comedy* by Dante, yet another Florentine.

Brunelleschi's dome on Florence's cathedral shows ancient Roman stylistic influence. Michelangelo patterned his dome for Saint Peter's in Rome after Brunelleschi's Florentine masterpiece.

Ghirlandaio's painting of the adoration of the Christ child by the shepherds. As was then the custom, only the principal figures were painted by Ghirlandaio. His students would have painted the background and minor figures.

This prosperity and the freedom from a central government may or may not have been the cause of Florence's creative spirit but it certainly supported it. The new wealth made an interest in learning and the arts possible. More people than ever before had the education, the money, and the time to enjoy painting, poetry, and sculpture. Much of the work of the Renaissance, including that of Michelangelo, was created only because there were those with fortunes large enough to pay for it.

Artists were in great demand. Although they depended on wealthy patrons to buy their works, they were considered extraordinary men with special talents and were treated with respect and awe. No longer were they thought of as little different from carpenters or stonecutters.

Ghirlandaio

Domenico Ghirlandaio was an artist typical of the quattrocento period (the 1400s) of the Renaissance. He specialized in large paintings of biblical scenes for the walls of private chapels of wealthy families. He painted to please the person paying the bills, and it was not unusual to find in these works a saint with the face of a wool merchant or a Madonna (the Virgin Mary) with the face of the merchant's daughter.

Ghirlandaio, like many busy, successful artists, painted only the most important parts of these works himself. He hired numerous assistants to do the rest—mix colors, prepare surfaces, and paint the backgrounds. In April 1488, Michelangelo was hired as the newest and youngest of these assistants.

3 Florence

As an apprentice to Ghirlandaio, Michelangelo was free to pursue his love of art, and a new world was open to him, one that went even beyond Ghirlandaio's studio. In his biography of Michelangelo, Charles de Tolnay wrote:

> Michelangelo's milieu [environment] from now on is no longer the dark, poor apartment in the Via dei Bentaccordi, but all Florence with its churches and palaces filled with ancient and modern art treasures . . . where the greatest artists of the centuries had continued to form a veritable museum of Tuscan sculpture. Here were the sculptured bronze doors of Andrea Pisano and of Ghiberti, and the marble statues of Donatello. Beyond that, his milieu is Florence, framed by hills and cut by the shining ribbon of the Arno, with its cubical buildings grouped around the mighty dome of Brunelleschi, its crystalline atmosphere so clear that even distant outlines are not dimmed. This world of pure abstract forms, where spirit seems to reign over matter, where a hidden geometry seems to underlie every form, is the true milieu in which Michelangelo is at home.[19]

To Michelangelo, Florence was like a pitcher of cold, calm, clear water to a thirsty man. He drank in the rich art that surrounded him.

His pen was as busy as his eyes. He was now free to draw instead of having to hide his work from his family. He sat for hours before the works of Giotto and Masaccio, making pen-and-ink copies. He drew his

Ghirlandaio was one of Florence's finest artists. He taught Michelangelo that drawing was the foundation of art.

The home of Dante, Giotto, Brunelleschi, and other masters, Florence provided Michelangelo with an environment rich in art.

fellow apprentices. He tried to get every detail perfect. Once, before copying a drawing showing some reptile-like demons tormenting a saint, he went to the marketplace to study fish so he could draw the demons' scales correctly.

Ghirlandaio encouraged Michelangelo and the other apprentices to draw constantly. Ghirlandaio was considered one of the best artists in Italy at capturing movement and emotion with his pen. Michelangelo learned from him that drawing was the foundation of all art, and aspects of Ghirlandaio's style are found in Michelangelo's work. Years later, Michelangelo wrote to a young assistant, "Draw, Antonio, draw, Antonio, draw—don't waste time!"[20]

Michelangelo painted as well as drew. Ghirlandaio specialized in the art form known as fresco, in which colors are applied to damp plaster. The colors mix with the plaster and, once the plaster dries, are bright and durable. Michelangelo learned the basics of mixing colors and applying them quickly before the plaster was too dry.

It was customary in Ghirlandaio's *bottega* or anywhere else for the youngest and newest apprentice to keep his eyes open and his mouth shut. The first was easy for Michelangelo; the second was not. He knew that his work, while far from being perfect, was better than that of his companions and perhaps better than Ghirlandaio's work.

Michelangelo's Talent and Arrogance

Michelangelo was not shy about pointing out to the other assistants their shortcomings. If he did not say the same thing in so many words to Ghirlandaio, he showed what he thought. Giorgio Vasari recorded

The Prodigy

Michelangelo, despite having had no formal training, displayed his talent quickly when apprenticed to Ghirlandaio. Giorgio Vasari, in The Lives of the Painters, Sculptors, and Architects, *describes these early efforts.*

"One day, while Domenico [Ghirlandaio] was engaged upon the large chapel of St. Maria Novella, Michelangelo drew the scaffolding and all the materials with some of the apprentices at work. When Domenico returned and saw it, he said, 'He knows more than I do,' and remained amazed at the new style produced by the judgment of so young a boy, which was equal to that of an artist of many years' experience. To this Michelangelo added study and diligence so that he made progress daily, as we see by a copy of a print engraved by Martin the German [Martin Schongauer], which brought him great renown. When a copper engraving by Martin of St. Anthony beaten by the devils reached Florence, Michelangelo made a pen drawing and then painted it. To counterfeit some strange forms of devils he bought fish with curiously coloured scales, and showed such ability that he won much credit and reputation."

one such incident:

Michelangelo's progress amazed Domenico [Ghirlandaio] when he saw him doing things beyond a boy, for he seemed likely not only to surpass the other pupils, of whom there were a great number, but would also frequently equal the master's own works. One of the youths happened one day to have made a pen sketch of draped women by his master. Michelangelo took the sheet and, with a thicker pen, made a new outline for one of the women, representing her as she should be and making her perfect. The difference between the two styles is as marvellous as the audacity of the youth whose good judgment led him to correct his master.[21]

Ascanio Condivi wrote that Ghirlandaio was jealous of his young apprentice and "gave him no help [taught him nothing] whatever."[22] It is very doubtful, however, that one of the most respected masters in Italy would be envious of a thirteen-year-old boy. It is more likely that Michelangelo, who never liked to admit to having learned anything from a fellow artist, exaggerated Ghirlandaio's jealousy in the stories he told to Condivi.

Whether or not he made his master envious, the arrogant, young Michelangelo was a somewhat troublesome assistant, despite his talent. Ghirlandaio was probably relieved when, after only one year, Michelangelo left the *bottega* for another opportunity. Lorenzo de' Medici, head of the richest and most powerful family in Florence and a patron of the arts, had established a school for young sculptors in the Medici gardens next to the monastery of San Marco. Lorenzo started the school because he worried that not enough young artists were becoming sculptors. The school was under the direction of the aged Bertoldo di Giovanni, who had been a pupil of the great Donatello.

Lorenzo asked several leading artists, including Ghirlandaio, to recommend candidates for the new school. Perhaps Ghirlandaio had seen in Michelangelo's drawings that he was better suited to sculpture than to painting. Maybe, he also saw a

Sketching the human body helped Michelangelo achieve perfect detail in his statues.

chance to rid himself of a problem. At any rate, Michelangelo, his friend Granacci, and a third apprentice went to Lorenzo's sculpture garden sometime late in 1489.

A Patron

It was not long before Michelangelo drew the attention of Lorenzo—*Il Magnifico*—himself. As Condivi told it, Michelangelo was copying in marble the head of an old satyr, a mythological creature that had the horns of a goat on a man's head, when Lorenzo strolled by. Condivi wrote:

> In the midst of this, the Magnificent, coming to see what point his works had reached, found the boy engaged in polishing the head and, approaching quite near, he was much amazed, considering first the excellence of the work and then the boy's age; and, although he did praise the work, nonetheless he joked with him as with a child and said, "Oh, you have made this satyr old and left him all his teeth. Don't you know that old men of that age are always missing a few?" To Michelangelo it seemed a thousand years before the Magnificent went away so that he could correct the mistake; and, when he was alone, he removed an upper tooth from his old man, drilling the gum as if it had come out with the root. . . . When he [Lorenzo] had come and noted the boy's goodness and simplicity, he laughed at him very much; but then, when he weighed in his mind the perfection of the thing and the age of the boy, he . . . resolved to help and encourage such great genius and to take him into his household.[23]

So it was that the fifteen-year-old Michelangelo went to live in one of the most splendid households in Italy. He was given a purple cloak (a sign of great favor) and a room of his own in the Medici palace. He often sat with Lorenzo's family at meals. His tutors were the scholars who taught Lorenzo's children.

One of these tutors, the philosopher Angelo Poliziano, greatly influenced Michelangelo. Poliziano was a Neoplatonist, one who combined the teachings of the ancient Greek philosopher Plato with Christianity. Neoplatonists believed that physical objects—mountains, trees, and even people—reflected the qualities of the God that created them. They thought truth was best found in beauty. This concept dominated Michelangelo's art for the rest of his life. To him, the human form was the ultimate in beauty—the perfect example of God's creation. The human body, especially the male nude, is the central theme in all of Michelangelo's works.

The subject of Michelangelo's first major work, *Battle of the Centaurs*, was suggested to him by Poliziano. It is a relief (carved on a single, flat surface rather than freestanding) showing a battle between men and centaurs, which are mythical half-man, half-horse beasts. In this piece, Michelangelo shows the power and movement he could bring forth from a marble block. Writer Robert Coughlan said that it was not a masterpiece, "but in its great vigor, its uninhibited use of the expressive nude and its venturesome handling of composition—all betokening originality, daring and skill developing at a very high speed—the *Centaurs* pointed to the greatness that lay not very far off."[24] Condivi wrote that Michelangelo, whenever he saw the *Centaurs* in later life, "realizes what a great wrong he committed

Young Michelangelo's first major work under Lorenzo de' Medici's patronage was a bas relief titled Battle of the Centaurs.

against nature by not promptly pursuing the art of sculpture"[25] and allowing himself to be sidetracked often into painting and architecture.

A Broken Nose

All was not perfect in the Medici garden, however. One day, Michelangelo let his criticism of a fellow student, Torrigiano, go too far. Vasari and Condivi claimed Torrigiano was envious, but Torrigiano's version, as told later to artist Benvenuto Cellini, is probably more correct.

> This Buonarroti and I used to go along together when we were boys to study in Masaccio's chapel at the church of the Carmine. Buonarroti had the habit of making fun of anyone else who was drawing there, and one day he provoked me so much that I lost my temper more than usual, and, clenching my fist, gave him such a punch on the nose that I felt the bone and cartilage crush like a biscuit. So that fellow will carry my signature until he dies.[26]

Michelangelo's nose was badly broken, and his face did, indeed, remain disfigured. The lover and creator of beauty had, he thought, been made ugly. Some biographers believe that this may have been the principal reason why Michelangelo remained depressed through much of his life.

Lorenzo de' Medici died in 1492, ending perhaps the happiest years of Michelangelo's life. Lorenzo's oldest son and heir, Piero, had never been friendly with Michelangelo, feeling unwelcome, moved

Perhaps the greatest art patron of the Renaissance, Lorenzo de' Medici recognized and nurtured Michelangelo's genius.

back to his own family's home.

The time Michelangelo spent away from the Medici family was one of the most important in his development as an artist, even though he undertook no works. Instead, he began to study human anatomy, dissecting corpses provided to him by the hospital at the monastery of Santo Spirito. He learned where muscles lie, how they are linked to each other and to bones, and how they contract to cause movement. This knowledge would make his sculpture more lifelike and full of action. Michelangelo was to become recognized as the master of the human form. Art historian Beatrice Farwell wrote, "Every later artist attempting heroic expression through the human body had to take him into account, and his influence was

Importance of the Nude

While in Lorenzo de' Medici's palace, Michelangelo came to feel that God's spirit was best reflected in the human body. Bernard Berenson, in The Italian Painters of the Renaissance, *tells why the nude is important to Michelangelo's work.*

"Now while it remains true that tactile [realistic] values can, as Giotto and Masaccio have forever established, be admirably rendered on the draped figure, yet drapery is a hindrance, and, at the best, only a way out of a difficulty, for we *feel* it masking the really significant, which is *the form underneath.* A mere painter, one who is satisfied to reproduce what everybody else sees. . .will scarcely comprehend this feeling. His only significant is the obvious—in a figure, the face and the clothing, as in most of the portraits manufactured nowadays. The artist, even when compelled to paint draped figures, will force the drapery to render the nude, in other words the material significance of the human body. But how much more clearly will this significance shine out, how much more convincingly will the character manifest itself, when between its perfect rendering and the artist nothing intervenes! And this perfect rendering is to be accomplished with the nude only. . . . We are now able to understand why every art whose chief preoccupation is the human figure must have the nude for its chief interest; why, also, the nude is the most absorbing problem of classic art at all times. . . . The first person since the great days of Greek sculpture to comprehend fully the identity of the nude with great figure art was Michelangelo."

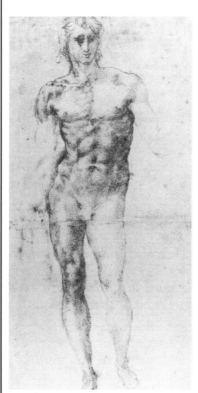

Michelangelo believed the nude figure represented the pinnacle of beauty and the greatest challenge to the artist.

still strong in the nineteenth century in the painting of Delacroix and Daumier and the sculpture of Rodin."[27] In gratitude for the opportunity to learn, Michelangelo carved for the head of the hospital a wooden figure of Christ on the cross.

In January 1494, Michelangelo returned to the Medici palace, summoned by Piero to do a special sculpture—a snowman. Piero was so pleased that he invited Michelangelo to live in the palace once more.

Michelangelo remained at the Medici palace only a few months. In August, King Charles VIII of France invaded Italy, conquered Genoa, and headed toward Florence. In October, with Piero's power crumbling and the French drawing near-

Original Sin *and other reliefs sculpted by Jacopo della Quercia were admired by Michelangelo in Bologna.*

French king Charles VIII invaded Italy in 1494, forcing Michelangelo to flee Florence.

er, Michelangelo fled to the city of Bologna. He remained there a year, under the protection of a city official, Gianfrancesco Aldovrandi. While in Bologna, Michelangelo admired and studied the sculpture of Jacopo della Quercia, especially the marble reliefs on the doorway of the church of San Petronio. The reliefs showed ten scenes from the Book of Genesis in the Bible. Michelangelo would paint some of the same scenes later in perhaps his most famous work, the ceiling of the Sistine Chapel.

Michelangelo won, with Aldovrandi's help, commissions, or contracts, to produce two sculptures for the tomb of Saint Dominic. They are considered among his lesser works and do not show the power of the *Centaurs.* Even so, as Michelangelo later told Condivi, the other sculptors in Bologna were jealous of the newcomer. Always ready to flee at signs of danger and probably homesick for Florence, Michelangelo went home toward the end of 1495.

In his absence, the Medici family had been run out of the city and their palace ransacked by a mob. Florence was controlled by the Popolari (the People's party) dominated by a friar, Girolamo Savonarola, who had preached against the nobility and corruption in the church. It was not a good time for artists, since Savonarola condemned all nonreligious art as frivolous. Nevertheless, Michelangelo was able to get a commission and Savonarola's approval to produce a statue of Saint John the Baptist for Lorenzo Popolano.

A Cupid Leads to a New Patron

After the statue was done, Michelangelo carved, apparently on his own, a statue of a sleeping cupid in the manner of ancient Rome. Popolano, a member of a branch of the Medici which, although friendly to Michelangelo, had opposed Piero, suggested Michelangelo make it look so much like an antique that it might be passed off as one and sold at a high price. Michelangelo agreed, and Popolano hired an art dealer, Baldassare del Milanese, to take the cupid to Rome. There, he sold it to a Cardinal Riario.

It is unclear whether Michelangelo set out to cheat the buyer of the cupid, but he was the one who wound up being cheated.

He received thirty ducats from the sale, but Cardinal Riario actually paid Baldassare two hundred ducats in the belief that the cupid was an ancient work.

The cardinal, however, later grew suspicious. He heard a rumor that the cupid had been made in Florence. He sent an agent there to look for the true artist. The agent eventually discovered Michelangelo. Condivi wrote:

> Then he [the agent] asked him [Michelangelo] if he had ever done any work in sculpture, and when Michelangelo said yes, that he had done, amongst other things an Eros [cupid] of such and such a height and pose, the gentleman found out what he wanted to know. And, after describing what had happened [the actual selling price], he promised Michelangelo that, if he were willing to go with him to Rome, he would help him to recover the difference and would set everything straight with his patron, whom he knew would be very pleased. Thus Michelangelo, partly out of anger at being defrauded and partly out of a desire to see Rome, which the gentleman had so extolled to him as offering the widest field for everyone to demonstrate his ability, went along with him and lodged in his house, which was near the cardinal's palace.[28]

And so, in June of 1496, the twenty-one-year-old Michelangelo first went to the city in which he would do some of his greatest work.

Chapter

4 A Great Sculptor

Michelangelo found Rome to be far different from the city that had been the capital of an ancient empire. Farmers now grazed their pigs in the Forum, and robbers lurked in the ruins of temples to pounce on unwary pilgrims. Still, the city was rich in ancient sculpture, and Michelangelo wasted no time in viewing it. Shortly after his arrival, he wrote to Popolano:

> I write this merely to inform you that on Saturday last we arrived here in safety and went immediately to visit the Cardinal di San Giorgio [Riario] . . . and he straightway expressed a desire that I should go and inspect certain statues. . . . On Sunday the Cardinal went to his new house and there caused me to be summoned. I went to him accordingly, and he asked my opinion of the statues I had seen. I told him what I thought, and certainly I consider that some of them are very beautiful. He then asked me if I had sufficient courage to undertake a beautiful work on my own account. I replied that I should not be able to produce any work equal to those I had been shown, but that I was willing he should see for himself what I could do. We have bought a piece of marble sufficiently large for a life-size figure, and on Monday I shall begin work on it.[29]

Some biographers of Michelangelo claim this statue was the *Bacchus*. Condivi, however, wrote that the artist "never

Michelangelo's first work completed in Rome was this statue of Bacchus, the Greek god of wine. It betrays an obvious classical influence yet adds an emotional component characteristic of the High Renaissance.

worked on any commission whatever from the cardinal"[30] and that the *Bacchus* was done for Jacopo Galli, a wealthy banker. Regardless, it is an important work. It shows both how the ancient statues influenced Michelangelo and how he improved on them. This slightly drunken god of wine, accompanied by a young satyr, stands in a typical antique pose—one knee forward—but seems about to fall over as a result of drinking from the cup in his right hand. Both faces show emotion. Bacchus is vacant and glassy-eyed, while the satyr grins mockingly. Howard Hibbard wrote that the spontaneity, grace, and design that mark the art of the High Renaissance (the period following the quattrocento) "are perhaps seen here for the first time in modern sculpture."[31]

The *Pietà*

An even more important work was just ahead. Galli, with whom Michelangelo was living, secured for him a commission from a French cardinal to carve a pietà, a figure of the Virgin Mary holding her dead son. Galli had such faith in his young guest that he guaranteed to the cardinal that the statue "shall be the finest work in marble which Rome today can show, and that no master of our days shall be able to produce a better."[32]

Michelangelo made good on Galli's guarantee. The *Pietà*, now one of the greatest treasures of the Vatican in Rome, is one of the world's most famous and best-loved works of art. Not only is the sculpture a technical masterpiece (a fold of Mary's robe is carved so thin that light shines through it) but it also appeals instantly to the viewer's emotions. Biographer Georg Brandes wrote, "At the age of twenty-four he [Michelangelo] had plumbed the abyss of sorrow in a single human soul."[33]

The *Pietà* was a sensation. People came from throughout Italy to see it. The artists of the time considered it virtually perfect. Vasari wrote that the *Pietà* "displays the utmost limits of sculpture."[34]

Michelangelo was proud of what he had done. Vasari wrote that the artist, standing near the *Pietà*, once overheard someone wonder aloud who the sculptor might be. He came to the chapel late that night, and on a band across Mary's chest, he carved the words "Michelangelo Buonarotti of Florence made this" in Latin. It was the only work he ever signed.

The *Pietà*, unlike much of Michelangelo's later work, is finished in every detail and highly polished. The figure of Christ shows how well the artist had learned his anatomy. The real importance of the *Pietà*, however, is in the reputation it brought to Michelangelo. He was now acknowledged as a master. "More than merely famous," wrote Robert Coughlan, "he was seen to be, without dissent, one of the surpassing artists of his time."[35]

Michelangelo became the main wage earner of the Buonarotti family. His father, who had continued to hold only minor government jobs, and his brothers depended on him for money. He sent it, although not always with good grace. On August 19, 1497, he wrote to his father:

I inform you that on Friday Buonarroto [a younger brother] arrived here. . . . He told me how you are getting along, and also that Consiglio the

The Pietà, one of the world's most famous works of art, is both technically perfect and emotionally compelling. If he had done no other work, its creation alone would have immortalized the name of Michelangelo.

merchant troubles you a great deal [about a debt]: that he is unwilling to settle on any sort of agreement and that he wants to have you arrested. I say that you must try to come to an understanding with him, and that you should advance him a few ducats; let me know what you agree to give him, and if you do not have that amount I shall send it to you. Though, as I told you, I have little money. I'll do my best to borrow some. . . . You must realize that I too spend money and have my own troubles. Just the same, I shall send you what you may ask of me, even if I have to sell myself as a slave.[36]

The needs of his family, the frustration of dealing with his patrons in Rome, and perhaps a touch of homesickness led Michelangelo to return to Florence in the spring of 1501. He had also received a challenging assignment that no sculptor could resist.

A New Commission Leads to *David*

In 1463, the sculptor Agostino di Duccio had been commissioned to carve a large statue for the Duomo, Florence's cathe-

Michelangelo's preliminary sketches for his master-piece David.

dral. He began work on an eighteen-foot block of white marble, then abandoned it. He had miscarved it so badly that it was considered unworkable and lay untouched for thirty-seven years.

In 1501, however, the cathedral board decided to try to have the marble sculpted again. A sculptor named Sansovino wanted the job badly. There was talk of giving the block to Leonardo da Vinci, even though Leonardo, honored as a painter, had never yet attempted sculpture. Some friends had written to Michelangelo in Rome about the situation, and shortly after his return to Florence, he requested and received the commission.

Michelangelo chose to carve the young David of the Bible. Or, rather, it was David whom he saw inside the huge block. Michelangelo believed that statues were imprisoned inside each block of marble. It was the artist's task to recognize what the block held and to liberate it. In one of his many poems, Michelangelo stated this view of sculpting:

> When godlike art has, with superior
>   thought,
> The limbs and motions in idea
>   conceived,
> A simple form, in humble clay
>   achieved,
> Is the first offering into being
>   brought;
> Then stroke on stroke from out the
>   living rock
> Its promised work the practised chisel
>   brings,
> And into life a form so graceful
>   springs,
> That none can fear for it time's rudest
>   shock.[37]

In another poem, he wrote:

Michelangelo usually followed his own creative spirit, refusing to listen to others. Vasari told of one time, however, when Michelangelo accepted a suggestion by his friend and patron Piero Soderini.

"Piero Soderini came to see it [the *David*], and expressed great pleasure to Michelangelo who was retouching it, though he [Soderini] said he thought the nose large. Michelangelo seeing [Soderini] below and knowing that he could not see properly, mounted the scaffolding and taking his chisel dexterously let a little marble dust fall on [Soderini] without, however, actually altering his work. Looking down he said, 'Look now.' 'I like it better,' said [Soderini], 'you have given it life.' Michelangelo therefore came down with feelings of pity for those who wish to seem to understand matters of which they know nothing."

Nothing the greatest artist can conceive
That every marble block doth not confine
Within itself; and only its design
The hand that follows intellect can achieve.[38]

Michelangelo began work in September 1501 in a large shed near the cathedral. As usual, he worked completely alone. He could never, especially later in his career, tolerate spectators or visitors. Sometimes, he was very reluctant to allow even a pope to see an unfinished work. He rarely used assistants and then only when absolutely necessary and for as short a time as possible. Some biographers say that Michelangelo was jealous and could not bear to have anyone with real talent around him. Others say he could never find pupils talented enough. Condivi said Michelangelo's lifelong tendency toward solitude was part of the creative process.

While he was young, then, Michelangelo dedicated himself not only to sculpture and painting but also to all those subjects that are pertinent or related to them; and this he did with such great application that for a time he all but withdrew from the company of men, frequently only a very few. As a result he was considered arrogant by some and, by others, bizarre and eccentric, although he had neither one vice nor the other, but . . . the love and continual practice of *virtù* [achievement] made him solitary and afforded him such delight and fulfillment that the company of others not only failed to satisfy him but even distressed him, as if it distracted him from his meditation, whereas he was never . . . less alone than when he was alone.[39]

The *David* was completed early in 1504

and was immediately considered a city treasure, a symbol of Florentine liberty. A committee of distinguished citizens was formed to decide where the statue would stand. It was unveiled outside the city hall on September 8, and as Coughlan wrote, "Florence was dazzled. Michelangelo was already famous. At this point he became more: he was incontestably the greatest sculptor in Italy."[40]

The High Renaissance

The chief importance of the *David* is that it was believed to point the way toward a new age in art. Coughlan wrote that the *David*, along with some of Leonardo da Vinci's works done about the same time, marked the end of the quattrocento and the beginning of the High Renaissance. Artists were no longer contented to portray people and objects naturally and realistically. Instead, they now tried to make each work express a feeling or spirit. Howard Hibbard wrote, "This [the *David*] is the first wholly successful union of antique inspiration with the new Florentine celebration of man; and from the time of its unveiling it was understood as the beginning of a new epoch in art."[41]

Most Renaissance artists had shown David in a victorious pose, with one foot on Goliath's bloody head. Michelangelo's David, however, is presented in the moment just before the battle. He is ready for action, his sling over his left shoulder. His body is tense. His expression is confident. He is, many experts think, a sort of spiritual self-portrait of Michelangelo. For one of the few times in his life, Michelangelo was completely confident in his ability and ready to take

David *is considered by art historians to herald the end of the quattrocento period and the start of the High Renaissance.*

This engraving from an 1873 edition of Illustrated London News *shows the huge proportions of Michelangelo's* David *as it is moved along railroad tracks.*

on any challenge. On one of the drawings for the *David*, he had written, "David with the sling, and I with the bow." The bow referred to a drill used on marble. Michelangelo, too, was ready to battle giants.

Leonardo Versus Michelangelo

Michelangelo's battle was fought not on a field but in Florence's city hall council room. The council decided to commission two huge murals, each a heroic scene from Florentine history. In February 1504, Leonardo da Vinci was chosen to do one. In August, Piero Soderini, head of the

council and the person most responsible for obtaining the *David* contract for Michelangelo, suggested that Michelangelo do the other side.

Michelangelo could not resist the challenge. Leonardo was his only true rival. In addition to being considered the best painter in Italy, Leonardo was handsome, witty, scholarly, and charming—everything Michelangelo was not. Leonardo thought painting far superior to sculpture and wrote:

This [sculpture] is a most mechanical exercise accompanied many times with a great deal of sweat, which combines with dust and turns into mud. The sculptor's face is covered with paste and all powdered with marble

Leonardo's self-portrait. Only da Vinci's genius could rival that of Michelangelo.

angelo. Leonardo was not just a talented rival; he was an enemy. One day, a group discussing a passage by the writer Dante asked Leonardo for his opinion. Michelangelo happened to be passing by, and Leonardo graciously asked his views on the verses. Michelangelo ignored the question. Instead, he used the opportunity to make a jab at Leonardo. He knew that Leonardo recently had failed to cast a statue of a horse in bronze and exclaimed, "Explain the question yourself, you who tried to make a bronze equestrian statue and couldn't. Only those asses in Milan would have thought you could!"[43]

Battle of Cascina

Although Leonardo's attempt at a bronze horse had failed, he was, in fact, an expert on painting horses. He chose as the subject for his mural the famous cavalry encounter at the Battle of Anghiari between Florence and Pisa in 1440. Michelangelo, too, picked a topic that reflected his artistic interest. He chose a moment before the Battle of Cascina, also between Florence and Pisa, in 1364. Florentine troops, bathing in a river, heard the battle alarm and scrambled out of the water seeking their clothes, armor, and weapons. It was a perfect opportunity for Michelangelo to show his specialty—portraying the nude, male body.

Michelangelo began work on the cartoon, which is a full-size, detailed drawing, for the *Battle of Cascina* in October, eight months after Leonardo. He worked night and day. Years later, Condivi described the way Michelangelo lived and worked.

Michelangelo has always been very ab-

dust, so that he looks like a baker, and he is covered with minute chips, so that he looks as though he had been out in the snow. His house is dirty and filled with chips and dust of stones. . . . We may say that just the opposite happens to the painter, since the well-dressed painter sits at great ease in front of his work, and moves a very light brush, which bears attractive colors. . . . His dwelling is full of fine paintings and is clean and often filled with music . . . unmixed with the pounding of hammers or other noises.[42]

Leonardo's attitude infuriated Michel-

Painting Versus Sculpture

Leonardo da Vinci, in his Treatise on Painting, *angered Michelangelo by writing that sculpture was far inferior to painting.*

"There is no comparison between the mental effort, amount of skill, and analysis required in painting and that required in sculpture. In sculpture there is no difficulty with perspective, because of the limitations of the material, and not because of the artificer. If the sculptor says that he cannot replace the material taken away from the stone that covers his work as the painter can replace parts of his work, the reply here is that he who takes away too much, understands too little and is not a master, for if he has control of the measurements of his work he will not remove what he ought not, and so we shall say that such a defect is in the master and not in his material. But painting is a marvelous artifice, based on most subtle observations, of which sculpture is wholly devoid since it involves only brief analysis. The reply to the sculptor who says that his science is more permanent than painting is that the permanence belongs to the material of which sculpture is composed and not to the sculptor. The sculptor ought not to claim this as his glory, but leave it to nature which created the material."

stemious [not indulgent] in his way of life, taking food more out of necessity than for pleasure, and especially while he had work in progress, when he would most often content himself with a piece of bread which he would eat while working. . . . And just as he has eaten sparingly, so also he has done with little sleep, since sleep, according to him, has seldom done him good. . . . When he was more robust, he often slept in his clothes and in the boots which he has always worn . . . and he has sometimes gone so long without taking them off that then the skin came away like a snake's with the boots.[44]

Leonardo finished his cartoon and began to paint in the spring of 1505. Typically, however, he experimented with new materials. The new type of paint he chose changed colors, and some of it even failed to stick to the wall, running down in streaks. The wall was ruined, and Leonardo abandoned the entire project.

Leonardo's failure did not result in a victory for Michelangelo, however. Before he could even finish his cartoon, Michelangelo was ordered to Rome in March 1505 by the former Pope Julius II, Cardinal Giuliano della Rovere, to create his tomb.

Cascina Influences Other Artists

The *Battle of Cascina*, though it was never finished, was possibly Michelangelo's most important work. For years, the cartoon, along with that of Leonardo's *Battle of Anghiari*, remained on display in Florence. A steady stream of artists came to admire and to copy them. Vasari called Michelangelo's cartoon a "school for artists" and named a dozen who visited, including the young Raphael, later to become another great rival of Michelangelo.[45] Benvenuto Cellini was only a boy at the time, but he later remembered the cartoons well and wrote, "So long as they remained intact, they were the school of the world."[46]

Neither, however, remained intact. No one knows what happened to Leonardo's. According to Vasari, Michelangelo's cartoon "was taken to the great hall of the Medici palace, where it was entrusted too freely to artists, for during the illness of Duke Giuliano it was unexpectedly torn to pieces and scattered in many places, some fragments still being in the house of . . . a Mantuan noble, where they are regarded with great reverence, indeed they are more divine than human."[47] Another version is

Michelangelo's cartoon, or preliminary drawing, of the Battle of Cascina *is thought by some experts to be his best work. It led to a new artistic style called mannerism. The photo below is an artist's copy of Michelangelo's drawing.*

Painting with the Head

Michelangelo, in a conversation recounted by Francisco de Hollanda and taken from Michelangelo: A Self-Portrait, *gave his opinion that painting is a function of the intellect as well as the hands.*

"In many places there are painters who are not painters, but as the majority of people are without sense and always love that which they ought to abhor, and blame that which deserves most praise, it is not very surprising that they are so constantly mistaken about painting, an art worthy only of great understandings, because without any discretion or reason, and without making any distinction, they call a 'painter' both the person who has nothing more than the oils and brushes of painting and the illustrious painter born only in the course of many years (which I consider to be a very great event); and as there are some who are called painters and are not painters, so there is also painting which is not painting, for they do it. And what is marvelous is that a bad painter neither can nor knows how to imagine, nor does he even desire to do good painting; his work mostly differs but little from his imagination, which is generally somewhat worse; for if he knew how to imagine well or in a masterly manner in his fantasy, he could not have a hand so corrupt as not to show some part or indication of his good will. But no one has ever known how to aspire well in this science, except the mind which understands what good work is, and what he can make of it. It is a serious thing, this distance and difference which exist between the high and the low understanding in painting."

that during a riot, the artists of Florence, afraid that the cartoon would be destroyed, divided it among themselves. At any rate, no piece survived, and the work is known today only from copies made by other artists.

Those copies show a change in Michelangelo's style, and this change would influence art for all time. In the *David*, he had used his knowledge of human anatomy to show action and emotion. In the *Battle of Cascina*, he went further. Muscles are exaggerated almost abnormally, and bodies are twisted to the extreme. Howard Hibbard wrote that Michelangelo's achievement "was to create a composition that would enable succeeding artists to use the human body in every possible position, with a freedom that had heretofore been lacking."[48]

The Battle Cartoon

Benvenuto Cellini, the famous goldsmith, was one of several artists who came to Florence to study Michelangelo's Battle of Cascina *cartoon. In his autobiography, Cellini gave his opinion that it was a better work than the Sistine ceiling.*

"In the course of conversation he happened to mention Michelangelo Buonarroti, led thereto by a drawing I had made from a cartoon of that divinest painter. This cartoon was the first masterpiece which Michelangelo exhibited, in proof of his stupendous talents. He produced it in competition with another painter, Leonardo da Vinci, who also made a cartoon; and both were intended for the council-hall in the palace of the Signory. They represented the taking of Pisa by the Florentines; and our admirable Leonardo had chosen to depict a battle of horses, with the capture of some standards, in as divine a style as could possibly be imagined. Michelangelo in his cartoon portrayed a number of foot-soldiers, who, the season being summer, had gone to bathe in the Arno. He drew them at the very moment the alarm sounded, and the men all naked run to arms; so splendid in their action that nothing survives of ancient or of modern art that touches the same lofty point of excellence; and as I have already said, the design of the great Leonardo was itself most admirably beautiful. These two cartoons stood, one in the palace of the Medici, the other in the hall of the Pope. So long as they remained intact, they were the school of the world. Though the divine Michelangelo in later life finished that great chapel of Pope Julius [the Sistine Chapel], he never rose halfway to the same pitch of power; his genius never afterwards attained to the force of those first studies."

Mannerism

The *Battle of Cascina* and Michelangelo's later works in the same style led to entirely new concepts of painting. One group of artists would go to greater extremes in distorting the human body and exaggerating movement. Each one tried to find an individual *maniera*, or style, and this type of art became known as Mannerism. Mannerism would flourish for the next hundred years, up to the time of El Greco in Spain in the early 1600s. Mannerists have been criticized, however, as showing movement for its own sake and neglecting spirit and emo-

Sketches in preparation for the Battle of Cascina. *The piece allowed Michelangelo to indulge in his love of depicting the human body in motion.*

tion. Even Leonardo saw this danger when he wrote, perhaps about Michelangelo: "O anatomical painter, beware, lest in the attempt to make your nudes display all their emotions by a too strong indication of bones, sinews, and muscles, you become a wooden [unimaginative] painter."[49]

Another group of artists, following Michelangelo, began to emphasize emotions more. This type of art came to be called Baroque. Some of the more famous followers of the Baroque style were Rubens, Murillo, Caravaggio, and Rembrandt.

Both art and Michelangelo had taken a new direction. Brandes wrote that the *Battle of Cascina* cartoon "marks the close of an epoch [period of time]. . . . It has been called the . . . dividing line between his first style and his second. . . . This car-

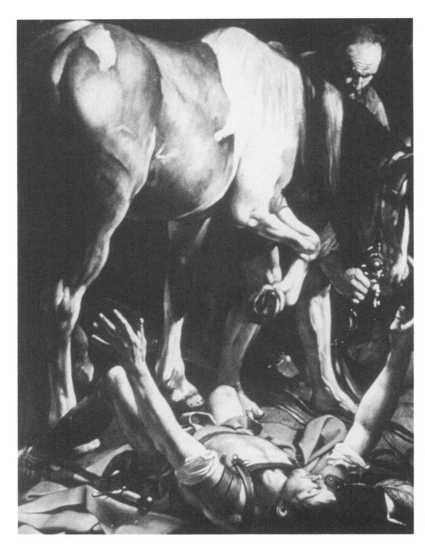

Caravaggio's Conversion of St. Paul *expresses the intense emotion of the Baroque style.*

toon, then, destined to perish so completely that not one scrap of it has survived, became the model for a whole generation of art students."[50] And biographer Marcel Brion wrote, "The whole of the Baroque is contained in the Cascina cartoon. . . . Michelangelo brought an esthetic period [the quattrocento] to an end; having developed all its resources. He now inaugurated a new epoch . . . with his dar-ing, his intuition, and his mistakes."[51]

The *Battle of Cascina*, for all its fame, is considered to be more a drawing by a sculptor than the work of a painter. Michelangelo, in fact, always considered himself a sculptor, not a painter. He could not have realized when he obeyed the summons of Pope Julius that he would soon undertake what was to become one of the most famous paintings in the world.

Chapter

5 The Sistine Chapel

Pope Julius II was, in many ways, the most central character in Michelangelo's life. In the eight years he served the pope, Michelangelo changed the course of painting and shifted the center of the Renais-

Pope Julius II was a central figure in Michelangelo's life. He commissioned one of Michelangelo's greatest achievements, the famed frescoes on the ceiling of the Sistine Chapel.

sance from Florence to Rome. Even in death, Julius would dominate Michelangelo's career. The pope's tomb would eventually cost Michelangelo more than forty years of his life spent in numerous lawsuits and a flood of bitterness.

During the Middle Ages, popes had come under the domination of the kings of France, and they actually resided in France from 1305 to 1378. When the Papacy moved back to Italy, the large area of central Italy it once governed had been taken over by various city-states and by numerous local rulers. Julius was one of a series of popes determined to regain control of these "papal states" and the revenue they brought in.

Julius was even more determined than most. Other popes had employed armies to regain this territory, but Julius put on armor and rode at the head of his own troops. Others had wanted the Papacy to rule Italy, but Julius wanted to make Rome the capital of Europe. His faith in himself was so sure that even before he won a single victory, he was thinking of building his tomb. He wanted it to equal those of the Roman emperors.

Michelangelo, after months of thought and sketching, presented a design that pleased the pope. The tomb would be enormous—a freestanding structure twenty-four feet wide, thirty-six feet deep, and almost thirty feet tall. Statues of bound prisoners representing the pope's victories and of the arts and sciences were to go around the first level. On the second were to be four large statues—Moses, Saint Paul, and two representing the active and the contemplative life. On the top level would be Julius's sarcophagus, or casket, supported by statues representing heaven and earth. Michelangelo projected that the tomb would have forty life-size statues, which would have required a lifetime of work.

Unfinished Work a Habit

It was not the first time nor would it be the last that Michelangelo allowed his creative genius to exceed what he could realistically accomplish. Just before he began work on the *David*, for example, he signed a contract for a series of fifteen statues of saints for a tomb in the city of Siena. Only one, Saint Matthew, was even roughed out of marble. Throughout his life, Michelangelo agreed to do much more work than was humanly possible. Many of these works were never started. Dozens of others were never finished.

Michelangelo, in fact, left more unfinished than finished work. There are various explanations, including that he simply took on too many assignments. Coughlan explained that Michelangelo possessed

> both an excessive optimism and a deep strain of melancholy. The optimism showed itself in the grandeur of his artistic ambitions and conceptions [exemplified in the *David*] and in his will-

Michelangelo's preliminary sketches for Julius II's tomb.

> ingness to take on the most challenging and time-consuming projects. He was full of confidence in his powers, full of eagerness to demonstrate them to his fellow artists, his city and the world. . . . His appetite for fame and his belief that he could accomplish whatever he set his mind to do were normal attributes of Renaissance man. But in his case they were linked with an abnormal unwillingness or inability to face the fact that even he had only a certain amount of time and energy. So he was forever pressed, falling behind, failing his patrons, failing himself; and this was in turn one of the abiding sources of his melancholy.[52]

Other art historians argue that since Michelangelo saw his task as one of liberating statues trapped inside blocks of marble, he stopped working on statues once he considered them free. He saw no need for finishing and polishing. Another theory is that Michelangelo's imagination was so full of ideas that he quickly grew bored with one and moved on to another. Brandes said that "his mind was overwhelmed with work and his mind was ever restless and tempestuous. Time and again one project would crowd out another."[53]

Vasari believed that Michelangelo left

Michelangelo left this and many more statues unfinished.

work unfinished because of his constant search for perfection. He wrote that Michelangelo's judgment

> was so severe that he was never content with anything he did. . . . For Michelangelo used to say that if he had had to be satisfied with what he did, then he would have sent out very few statues, or rather none at all. This was because he had so developed his art and judgment that when on revealing one of his figures he saw the slightest error he would abandon it and run to start working on another block, trusting that it would not happen again.[54]

Whatever the reason for Michelangelo's overconfidence, it was shared by Julius, who was delighted with the tomb's ambitious design. The artist signed a contract, was given a sum of money, and went to Carrara for eight months to select blocks of marble. Early in 1506, the first blocks arrived in Rome. Michelangelo set up his shop in a house near Saint Peter's Church. As Michelangelo worked, the pope often visited him. Julius even ordered a corridor built between his lodgings and Michelangelo's studio so that he could go in secret.

Saint Peter's Versus the Tomb

The pope had decided that the only suitable place for the new tomb was a new basilica, or large central area, for Saint Peter's. Sangallo, the pope's architect, submitted a design, but Julius preferred another by Donato Bramante and made him chief architect in Sangallo's place. Bra-

The Solitary Worker

"Michelangelo formed no school, and was incapable of confiding the execution of his designs to any subordinates. This is also a point of the highest importance to insist upon. Had he been other than he was . . . he might have sent out [used other artists to paint] all those twelve Apostles for the Duomo from his workshop. Raffaello [Raphael] would have done so; indeed, the work which bears his name in Rome could not have existed except under these conditions. . . . Michelangelo was unwilling or unable to organize a band of craftsmen fairly interpretative of his manner. When his own hand failed, or when he lost the passion for his labor, he left the thing unfinished. And much of this incompleteness in his life-work seems to me due to his being what I called a dreamer. He lacked the merely business faculty, the power of utilizing hands and brains. He could not bring his genius into open market, and stamp inferior productions with his countersign. Willingly he retired into the solitude of his own self, to commune with great poets and to meditate upon high thoughts, while he indulged the emotions arising from forms of strength and beauty presented to his gaze upon the pathway of experience."

mante, however, was jealous of Michelangelo. He wanted Saint Peter's to be uppermost in Julius's mind and set out to end the close relationship between the pope and Michelangelo.

As Michelangelo told Condivi, Bramante began to convince the pope that it was bad luck to build a tomb during one's lifetime. Whether the pope believed Bramante or not, Julius stopped visiting Michelangelo and became more interested in Saint Peter's. Michelangelo began

having trouble getting in to see the pope or getting money to pay for materials and assistants.

One Saturday in April 1506, Michelangelo went to plead with the pope for money. Waiting his turn, he heard the pope say to a jeweler (but obviously so that Michelangelo would hear) that he would not spend any more for stones, large or small, an obvious reference to Michelangelo's plight. When he was finally able to talk to the pope, Julius told him to come back on

Donato Bramante designed Saint Peter's Church for Pope Julius II.

Monday. Michelangelo went on Monday, Tuesday, Wednesday, and Thursday with no result. He wrote more than thirty years later what happened when he went on Friday.

> One morning when I was there to talk about finances, he [the pope] had me turned away by a lackey. As a bishop from Lucca who was witness to the incident said to the lackey: "Don't you recognize this man?" The lackey said to me, "Pardon me, sire, but I am ordered to act thus." I returned home and wrote as follows to the pope: "Most Blessed Father, I have this morning been expelled from the Palace on orders from your Holiness; therefore I am advising you that from now on, if you wish me, you will seek for me elsewhere than in Rome."[55]

Michelangelo's pride had been sorely wounded. He left Rome for Florence.

Julius, angry that Michelangelo had left without his permission, sent horsemen to bring him back. By the time they reached him, however, he was in Florentine territory where the pope had less authority. The battle of wills went on for seven months. Julius repeatedly ordered Michelangelo back to Rome. Michelangelo replied that he would return only if the pope fulfilled his contract for the tomb.

Julius then began to threaten Florence with war if the city did not turn over the rebellious artist. Michelangelo's good friend Soderini called him in and, according to Condivi, said, "You have tried the [patience of the] pope as a king of France

Michelangelo was a proud, stubborn man who would be cowed by no one—even a pope. A rebuff by Julius II angered the artist so much that he left Rome and refused to return.

God's Terrible Vicar

Pope Julius II, both in life and after his death, had a great impact on Michelangelo. In The Life of Michelangelo Buonarroti, *John Addington Symonds describes this warrior-priest.*

"This man possessed a fiery temper, indomitable energy, and the combative instinct which takes delight in fighting for its own sake. Nature intended him for a warrior; and, though circumstances made him chief of the church, he discharged his duties as a Pontiff in the spirit of a general and a conqueror. . . . There was nothing petty or mean in Julius II; his very faults bore a grandiose and heroic aspect. Turbulent, impatient, inordinate in his ambition, reckless in his choice of means, prolific of immense projects, for which a lifetime would have been too short, he filled the ten years of his pontificate with a din of incoherent deeds and vast schemes half accomplished. Such was the man who called Michelangelo to Rome at the commencement of 1505. . . . Between the two men there existed a strong bond of sympathy due to community of temperament. Both aimed at colossal achievements in their respective fields of action. The imagination of both was fired by large and simple rather than luxurious and subtle thoughts. . . . Both worked with what the Italians call fury, with the impetuosity of demonic natures; and both left the impress of their individuality stamped indelibly upon their age."

would not have done. However, he is not to be kept begging any longer. We do not want to go to war with him over you and place our state in jeopardy. Therefore, make ready to return."[56] Michelangelo said that rather than return to the pope, he would flee to Turkey to work for the sultan. It took some months and a series of letters in a calmer tone from Julius, but Soderini finally convinced Michelangelo to make peace with the pope.

In November, Michelangelo went to Bologna, which had just surrendered to the pope and his army. He was taken to Julius, wearing a rope around his neck as a sign of repentance. As Vasari reported:

He knelt before the pope, who looked wrathfully at him, and said as if in anger: "Instead of coming to us, you have waited for us to come and find you." Michelangelo spread his hands and humbly asked for pardon in a loud voice, saying he had acted in anger through being driven away, and that he hoped for forgiveness for his error. The bishop who presented him

[Michelangelo] made excuses, saying that such men are ignorant of everything except their art. At this the pope waxed wroth [became angry], and striking the bishop with a mace he was holding, said: "It is you who are ignorant, to reproach him when we say nothing." The bishop therefore was hustled out by the attendants, and the pope's anger being appeased, he blessed Michelangelo.[57]

Michelangelo may have thought he would resume work on the tomb, but Julius commissioned a large bronze statue of himself instead. Michelangelo did a model of the pope giving a blessing with his right hand. When Michelangelo asked if the left hand should hold a book, Julius said, "What book? A sword; because I for my part know nothing about letters."[58] The ten-foot-high bronze was completed in February 1508 and placed over the main door of the cathedral in Bologna, perhaps as a reminder to the rebellious citizens. Only three years later, the people revolted again, and the statue was melted down and cast as a cannon, which was mockingly named *La Giulia* (Little Julius).

The Sistine Chapel

Michelangelo returned to Florence but stayed only until March. He was again summoned to Rome by Julius, who had yet another project for him—to paint the ceiling of the Sistine Chapel. It is unclear what made the pope request this. Michelangelo always claimed it was Bramante's idea. Michelangelo thought Bramante was trying again to postpone the work on the tomb. He also believed that Bramante, who knew Michelangelo had little experience in painting, was destined to fail and thus advance young Raphael, a relative of Bramante. Condivi wrote that Michelangelo "who had not yet used colors and who realized that it was difficult to paint a vault, made every effort to get out of it, proposing Raphael and pleading that this was not his art and that he would not succeed; and he went on refusing to such an extent that the pope almost lost his temper."[59]

A rear view of the Sistine Chapel (top) in the papal palace in the Vatican.

"It is not my art"—*Non era mia arte*—is a phrase Michelangelo used again and again throughout his life. It was his standard protest against doing anything—painting, bronzes, poetry, architecture—except sculpture. The protest did him no good. The pope would have his way. Michelangelo finally yielded but continued to make his point even when he signed a receipt on May 10, 1508, writing, "I, Michelangelo Buonarroti, sculptor, have received from his Holiness 500 ducats . . . for the paintings of the vault of the Chapel of Pope Sixtus [Sistine Chapel]."[60]

Sixtus IV, who built the Sistine Chapel in 1473, was the uncle of Pope Julius. Frescoes by some of Italy's most famous artists—including Michelangelo's first master, Ghirlandaio—adorned the chapel's walls. The high, curved ceiling, however, was painted a pale blue and decorated with stars.

Julius's idea was to divide the center of the ceiling into twelve sections, each containing a painting of one of Jesus's disciples. But Michelangelo, despite being unwilling to undertake the job in the first place, proposed something far grander. He would paint nine scenes from the Book of Genesis down the center, surrounding them with prophets and sibyls (legendary female prophets), plus an Old Testament scene in each corner. So, instead of twelve figures in the center of the ceiling, Michelangelo committed himself to hundreds of figures covering the entire surface down to the windows.

Michelangelo began by rejecting the scaffolding Bramante had built, which would have left holes in the ceiling when the work was done. He built one of his own, a freestanding structure that gave hints of his later abilities as an architect. Since his only experience at fresco had been during his year with Ghirlandaio, he hired four assistants from Florence, including his old friend, Granacci.

They started with the scene depicting doomed sinners trying to save themselves

Two of Michelangelo's sketches for figures painted in the Sistine Chapel show his concern for the smallest details of anatomy.

The ceiling of the Sistine Chapel. Michelangelo, with little assistance, took four years to complete the stunning array of frescoes depicting scenes from the Book of Genesis surrounded by Hebrew and pagan prophets.

from rising water as Noah's ark floats in the background. Michelangelo did the cartoon, and the assistants transferred it to the ceiling and began applying the colors. But Michelangelo, as always, disliked working with others. He found fault with the work of his assistants and wanted to do everything himself. One day, the assistants came to the chapel and found the doors locked. Not wishing to dismiss them in person, Michelangelo had simply shut them out. He would finish the entire ceiling by himself, taking four years to do so.

His early attempts were disastrous. The colors ran and mildewed. Michelangelo tried to use this as an excuse to abandon the entire project. "Indeed I told Your Holiness that this is not my art; what I have done is spoiled," he said to the pope. "If you do not believe it, send someone to see."[61] The pope sent an expert who soon discovered that Michelangelo had used too wet a plaster. He was forced to continue.

Michelangelo made other mistakes. In his first few scenes, he failed to consider that they would be viewed from sixty feet below. As a result, the figures are too small to be seen in detail. He realized his error and made later scenes less crowded and the figures larger.

More important, his style of painting developed as he worked. The early portions have been called "the creations of a painter coming from sculpture."[62] They have the look of a carved relief. The later scenes, however, such as the ones depicting the creation of Adam and the creation of the universe, show that Michelangelo not only learned the lessons of perspective and chiaroscuro from Giotto and Masaccio but had taken these techniques to new heights.

(Right) The Sistine Chapel and one of its famous frescoes, the Creation of Adam (above).

Michelangelo wanted to work in solitude, but there was one visitor he could not keep away. Pope Julius, well into his sixties, would come in the evening and climb the sixty feet of ladders to the scaffolding to check Michelangelo's progress. This progress was never fast enough to suit the pope. "When will you finish?" he repeatedly asked. "When I can" was always the abrupt reply.[63]

This was an example of what those who knew Michelangelo called his *terribilitá*, a combination of stubborness, short temper, and enormous talent. To the Italians, it meant "powerful" or "intense" rather than something to inspire terror. A later pope would say, "But, you see, Michelangelo is *terrible*, and there is no

The Impact of the Sistine Ceiling

Michelangelo's painting on the Sistine Chapel ceiling is stunning both in size and subject matter. In his book Michelangelo, *Charles de Tolnay describes the impact on the viewer.*

"The ceiling is a symphony of human forms. They are co-ordinated or subordinated, superimposed and rhythmic, on different scales from giant to child, some naked, some clothed, in marble, bronze or flesh—forms which present themselves in isolation or in groups, acting simultaneously, sometimes jostling each other in a seething mass, but always dominated by the strict lines of the architectonic [architectural] framework. It is a sublime sight, this *fortissimo* [great strength] of movement which develops in a crescendo of waves towards the back of the Chapel, gripping the spectator who, even before he has grasped its meaning, feels the sensuous [appealing to the senses] thrill of annihilation in a higher world. In its constantly recurring movement, its mass, weight, and the resulting polyphony [multiple themes], this work can no longer be classified as belonging to the style of the High Renaissance, and yet neither does it belong to the Baroque with its continuous motion and melting forms. Here, everything remains clearly defined and the ensemble is powerfully rhythmic. The style is a personal one which Michelangelo has developed from that of the High Renaissance."

Noah's Ark and the Great Flood scene from the Sistine ceiling.

The Delphic oracle (left) of ancient Greece and the ancient Hebrew prophet Jonah are two of twelve prophets Michelangelo painted on the ceiling of the Sistine Chapel.

getting on with him."[64] This quality of enormous force was revealed on the Sistine ceiling and would be more apparent in later works.

In the spring of 1510, when the ceiling was less than half done, the pope insisted that the scaffolding be removed so that he could view the work from ground level. Michelangelo protested, but the pope was determined. Julius and, indeed, much of Rome crowded into the chapel to see the scenes. The pope was very pleased, but Michelangelo's enemies were not. They realized that it was a masterpiece. Bramante, Michelangelo would later claim, even asked the pope to dismiss Michelan-

gelo and allow Raphael to finish the ceiling. The pope, however, "daily became more convinced of Michelangelo's genius, and wished him to complete the work, judging that he would do the other half even better. Thus, single-handedly, he completed the work in twenty months."[65]

A Difficult Process

These twenty months were not happy ones. Michelangelo was bitter about having to abandon sculpture and his work on the tomb. He was convinced Bramante and Raphael were conspiring to ruin him.

He lived like a hermit, emerging from the Sistine Chapel only to beg Julius for more money. In 1508, he wrote that "for the last twelve years I have been drudging all over Italy; I have borne every shame; I have endured every hardship; I have lacerated my body with every sort of hard work; I have exposed my life to a thousand dangers."[66] And in 1511, in a sonnet to Pope Julius, he complained:

> To tales and foolish talk thou listenest still,
> Rewarding him [Bramante] who is truth's enemy.
> I am of old thy faithful servitor,
> To thee belong as to the sun its rays;
> But thou, unreckoning of my wasted days,
> Art more displeased, as I toil the more.[67]

Painting the Sistine ceiling was physically difficult as well. Michelangelo did not, as shown in a film version of his life, paint lying on his back or wear a paper hat with a candle stuck in it. He did, however, spend hour after hour bent backward, reaching up with his brush. At one point during his work, he wrote:

> In this hard toil I've such a goiter grown. . . .
> That chin and belly meet perforce in one.
> My beard doth point to heaven, my scalp its place
> Upon my shoulder finds; my chest, you'll say,
> A harpy's is, my paint brush all the day
> Doth drop a rich mosaic on my face.
> My loins have entered my paunch within,
> My nether end my balance doth supply,
> My feet unseen move to and fro in vain.
> In front to utmost length is stretched my skin
> And wrinkled upon in folds behind, while I
> Am bent as bowmen bend a bow in Spain.
> No longer true or sane,
> The judgment now doth from the mind proceed,
> For tis ill shooting through a twisted reed.[68]

At last the ceiling was completed, or almost completed. Michelangelo wanted to add a few final touches, but Julius threatened to throw him off the scaffolding if he did not finish immediately. Michelangelo bowed to the pope's will, and the chapel was opened on November 1, 1512. Vasari wrote, "The pope went there to sing Mass amid the enthusiasm of the whole city."[69] Later, the pope suggested to Michelangelo that the prophets' robes ought to be decorated with gold. "It [the ceiling] will look poor" otherwise, Julius complained. The artist answered, "Those who are depicted there, they were poor, too."[70]

The Sistine Ceiling Influences Others

The artists of the time realized immediately that this was a marvelous work of art. Vasari wrote, "This work has been a veritable beacon to our art. . . . Indeed, painters no longer care about . . . methods of new expression . . . because this work contains ev-

Raphael's masterpiece the Madonna of the Goldfinch *(left) imitates Michelangelo's Sistine Chapel frescoes.*

ery perfection that can be given. . . . O, happy age! O, blessed artists who have been able to refresh your darkened eyes at the fount of such clearness, and see difficulties made plain by this marvelous artist."[71]

Raphael heads a long list of artists whose work was influenced by the Sistine ceiling. Almost immediately, his painting became more like that of Michelangelo.

Brandes wrote that when Raphael subsequently painted a likeness of God, for instance, "he had no alternative but to walk in Michelangelo's footsteps."[72] Michelangelo was as jealous of Raphael as he had been of Leonardo. He sneeringly called Raphael the "troop commander" because he was usually surrounded by assistants and admirers. Raphael retorted that the solitary

The prophet Daniel as depicted by Michelangelo on the Sistine ceiling.

Michelangelo was "lonely as a hangman."[73] Michelangelo remained bitter at what he considered Raphael's theft of his ideas. Twenty-two years after Raphael's premature death at the age of thirty-seven, Michelangelo wrote, "All he had of art, he had from me."[74]

Perhaps the most important Sistine ceiling paintings for future artists were the twenty nude youths, or *ignudi*, that fill the spaces beside the biblical scenes. They provided and still provide the same inspiration for painting the human form as the earlier *Battle of Cascina* cartoon did. They are so compelling that Brandes wrote that Michelangelo "sometimes vests these his darlings with so much life of their own that they almost blanket his fine paintings. Ruthlessly they reach beyond the frames, showing little respect for the works of art they are meant to serve."[75]

The Sistine ceiling would lead artists to pursue new, different directions. Howard Hibbard wrote that it contains "qualities that we associate with Mannerism, a leading stylistic current of the succeeding years and one that Michelangelo was instrumental in creating."[76] He adds, however, that the powerful, emotion-filled characters such as the prophets Daniel and Jonah were to lead some artists in another direction. They would produce the romantic, emotional Baroque style of the 1600s. Many generations of artists would study and copy Michelangelo's figures. In 1784, a portrait by Englishman Joshua Reynolds was modeled after one of the Sistine prophets. The gestures of *The Sower*, produced by Jean-François Millet in 1860, were borrowed from the Sistine paintings. Michelangelo probably would not have been impressed with their imitations of his work. Once when he saw a group of young painters eagerly copying from the Sistine ceiling, Michelangelo said, "Oh, how many there are who want to make something clumsy of this work of mine."[77]

6 Breaking the Bonds and Chains of Tradition

Pope Julius was highly pleased with Michelangelo's work on the Sistine Chapel ceiling, but he did not have long to enjoy it. He died early in 1513, only four months after the ceiling was completed. Michelangelo met soon afterward with the pope's family, the della Rovere. They wanted Michelangelo to carve a tomb even more elaborate than the original design. It was supposed to be completed in seven years. It would actually take thirty-four years—years of frustration for Michelangelo—before a much smaller version was finished.

Michelangelo set up his workshop in a house in Rome and worked almost uninterrupted on the tomb until 1517. Although he wrote his brother in July that he was "working so hard that I scarcely have time to eat,"[78] there was not much to show for the four years. Michelangelo lacked both the ability and the desire to organize a group of talented assistants, which was necessary for such a project. As usual, he wanted to do everything himself. He did not want artists with real ability helping him. He may also have lost some of the enthusiasm he had had for the project in 1505.

This period, however, produced the *Moses*, one of Michelangelo's most famous, and some say best, statues. The *Moses* was to sculpture what the Sistine ceiling was to painting. It equals the *Pietà* and the *David* in technical ability but is a far more intense work. Michelangelo gave Moses the same power and grandeur he gave to the

A painting depicts Michelangelo at work on his Moses.

Michelangelo's Moses *adorns the tomb of his patron Pope Julius II. Some believe the work elevated sculpture to new heights just as the Sistine ceiling had elevated painting.*

God of the Sistine ceiling. The statue has been interpreted in various ways. Some think it represents Pope Julius as Moses, angry at finding the children of Israel worshiping idols. Others say it is an expression of the artist's own *terribilitá*, "with all his hopes, all his knowledge, all his enthusiasms, and all his disappointments."[79] The important thing about the *Moses* is not what it means, but what it portrays—"an overwhelming surge of power not even re-motely equaled by any subsequent representation of Moses."[80]

The other two works done for the tomb at this time were even more important. These are the *Dying Slave* and the *Rebellious Slave*. They were intended to represent enemies conquered by the pope. Like *Moses*, they are figures from the Sistine ceiling carved in marble. In this case, the *ignudi* were used as models. The slaves' bodies are twisted as if fighting for free-

Moses

The Moses, *carved for the tomb of Pope Julius II, is considered by many to be Michelangelo's finest sculpture. Giovanni Zappi, writing years after Michelangelo's death, composed this sonnet that shows how it affected those who viewed it. The quote is taken from John Addington Symonds's biography.*

"Who is the man who, carved in this huge stone,
    Sits giant, all renowned things of art
    Transcending? He whose living lips, that start,
    Speak eager words? I hear, and take their tone.
He, sure, is Moses. That the chin hath shown
    By its dense honour, the brows' beam bipart:
    'Tis Moses, when he left the Mount, with part,
    A great part, of God's glory round him thrown.
Such was the prophet when those sounding vast
    Waters he held suspense about him; such
    When he the sea barred, made it gulph [swallow] his foe.
And you, his tribes, a vile calf did you cast?
    Why not an idol worth like this so much?
    To worship that had wrought you lesser woe.

dom. They are nowhere near as finished as the *Moses* and represent a change in Michelangelo's style. *Moses* is the last statue in which Michelangelo feels the need to display technical ability. The slaves point the way toward his later style in which he sought to break free of reality in order to show ideas. In his statues "from this time on, a personal vision transforms the prosaic [realistic portrayal] program."[81]

New Projects Interrupt Work on the Tomb

A new project from a new pope halted this work, however. After Julius's death, Giovanni de' Medici, the second son of Michelangelo's old patron Lorenzo, became pope and took the name Leo X. At first, Leo was satisfied to have Michelangelo working on Julius's tomb. Later, however, Leo lost his enthusiasm for a tomb honoring a member of a rival family.

In addition, Leo wanted Michelangelo to produce pieces for himself and the Medici family. Although he and Michelangelo had never been particularly close, Leo would later say, "Buonarroti and I were educated together under my father's roof."[82]

The new project was a façade, the exterior surface, for the Medici family church of San Lorenzo in Florence. Even though he had no experience in architecture, Michelangelo badly wanted the commission and wanted it all to himself. Per-

Michelangelo's Dying Slave *represented a change in his style.*

Michelangelo to the very great sorrow of both Michelangelo and the Cardinals. . . . So it came about that Michelangelo, weeping, left the tomb and went to Florence.[83]

This was not the only time that Michelangelo would portray himself as a helpless victim, even though letters and contracts tell a different story today.

The San Lorenzo project wasted three years of Michelangelo's life. The pope insisted that the marble come from the quarries at Pietrasanta, which had recently been bought by Florence, rather than from Carrara. This was extremely difficult because Michelangelo had to have a road built across the mountains to ship the

Giovanni de' Medici commissioned Michelangelo to create a façade for the de' Medici family church.

haps it was because Raphael was one of his rivals for the job. Michelangelo sent drawings to Leo, who granted him the commission in November 1516. In the meantime, perhaps with Leo's help, he got the della Rovere family to accept a new contract for a much smaller tomb for Julius.

Michelangelo would later give a much different version of this same negotiation. Condivi wrote that the artist

> put up all the resistance he could, alleging that he was under obligation [to the della Rovere cardinals] . . . and could not fail them. But the pope, who had resolved upon this, answered him, "Let me deal with them, for I shall see that they are satisfied." So he sent for them both and made them release

Anguish over the Tomb of Julius

Taken from Michelangelo: A Self-Portrait, this letter from Michelangelo to a representative of Pope Paul III shows what effect the continuing disagreements over the unfinished tomb of Pope Julius II had on the artist's work.

"Your Lordship has word sent to me that I am to paint and not have doubts about anything. I reply that one paints with the brain and not with the hands; and that he who cannot have his brain about him does himself a disservice; so until my affairs are arranged, I shall not do anything good. The rectification [correction] of the previous contract [with the heirs of Julius II] has not come; so long as the previous agreement is operative, drawn up under Clement [Pope Clement VII], I am stoned every day as though I had crucified Christ. I tell you that it was not my understanding that the aforesaid contract had the approval of Pope Clement. I say that the contract which I heard read before Pope Clement was not like the copy I afterward received. . . . I find myself having lost my youth and manhood, tied down to this tomb, which I defended as much as possible with Popes Leo and Clement; and my excessive loyalty which no one consented to acknowledge has ruined me. Thus my destiny wishes it! I see many men with incomes of 2,000 or 3,000 crowns lying in bed, while I with my very great efforts manage to grow poorer."

marble. Because of his inability to organize others, work on the road took far longer than planned. Then, much of the marble arrived in Florence damaged. In 1520, Pope Leo grew tired of the delays and canceled the contract.

Even though it was never built, the San Lorenzo façade was important because it helped develop Michelangelo's architectural style. Its style was not copied from Greece, Rome, or the Middle Ages. Instead, the design was "novel . . . a careful balance of horizontal and vertical . . . not simply a relief but truly three-dimensional. . . . As in so much of Michelangelo's work, ideas developed for one commission bore fruit in the next."[84]

The next commission came soon, and it would be far more successful. Pope Leo had not given up on Michelangelo. He looked for a project that would properly use the artist's talent and energy. Giuliano, the third son of Lorenzo the Magnificent, had died in 1516. Lorenzo's grandson, also named Lorenzo, died in 1519. Leo therefore decided to build a new chapel at San Lorenzo to be a tomb for these two young members of the fami-

Pope Clement VII, Michelangelo's childhood friend, understood the artist's moods.

ly as well as for the elder Lorenzo and his brother Giuliano. Michelangelo was asked to design the chapel and carve the statues.

Conflicts over the Tomb

Michelangelo worked on the chapel, with many interruptions, from 1520 to 1534. The first interruption came almost immediately when Pope Leo died in 1521. Leo's cousin, Cardinal Giulio de' Medici, stopped work on the project. The new pope, Adrian VI from the Netherlands, did not approve of "pagan" statues and, furthermore, was an ally of the della Rovere family. Michelangelo, threatened with a lawsuit by the della Rovere family, resumed work on the tomb of Julius, roughing out four figures—the so-called Florentine slaves. He would not work on the tomb for long, however. Adrian died after

only twenty months, and Giulio de' Medici became Pope Clement VII.

As a boy, Michelangelo had been closer to Giulio, who was three years younger, than to any of the other Medici children. As a result, Giulio, as pope, was much more sensitive than his predecessors to the artist's moods. He forgave Michelangelo for leaving major works unfinished as well as for minor shortcomings, such as not showing enough respect. "Whenever Buonarroti comes to see me," he once said, "I always ask him to sit down, because he certainly will, without leave or license."[85]

Troubles with the della Rovere Family Continue

Soon after becoming pope, Clement not only ordered Michelangelo to resume work on the Medici tomb but also added another project. This was the Laurentian Library, to be built next to San Lorenzo and to contain the Medici manuscript collection. Michelangelo was now caught between the demands of Clement and the lawsuit by the della Rovere family. He appealed to the pope, who got the della Rovere family to agree to a still smaller tomb.

It took Michelangelo a year to submit a new design for the smaller tomb. The della Rovere family rejected it, and the lawsuit continued. By now, the project, which had been Michelangelo's grand dream in 1505, had turned into a nightmare. He wrote to a friend:

> Maybe passion made me try to wield too big a stick. I've had recent information on how things are going down there [Rome] and this gave me quite a

fright. I refer to the ill disposition which Julius' relatives have taken toward me—and not without reason—and how the lawsuit is proceeding, demanding damages and interest, so that a hundred like myself couldn't give satisfaction. This has placed me in great travail and makes me wonder where I'd be if the pope failed me, since I'd no longer be in this world. . . . Now I only want what the pope wants; I know that he wishes neither my ruin nor my shame. . . . I want to get out of this obligation more than I want to go on living.[86]

The pope had his way. Michelangelo spent most of his time from 1524 to 1527 working on the Medici chapel and library. Then, the work was halted again, this time by war.

The Sack of Rome

For years, King Francis I of France and Charles V, who was both king of Spain and emperor of the Holy Roman Empire (made up mostly of modern-day Germany and Austria), had been fighting in northern Italy. Both claimed sovereignty over the same territory. By 1527, Charles had grown so much more powerful than Francis that Pope Clement worried that Charles would try to conquer all of Italy. Clement, therefore, made a secret treaty to go to war with France against Charles. Charles, however, learned of the alliance and struck first, sending an army to Italy. The army took Rome on May 6, 1527. Clement fled to a nearby castle while the conquering army burned and looted his city. Many

Charles V of Spain sent an army to Italy that sacked Rome and turned the Sistine Chapel into a stable.

art treasures were destroyed. The Sistine Chapel was turned into a stable.

The sack of Rome shocked Europe. Its brutality deeply affected the people of the time, and some historians believe it ended the Renaissance. People no longer believed in the nobility of man.

The incident had an immediate effect on Florence and Michelangelo. Florence, at this time, was governed by Cardinal Passerini, who was acting as guardian for two young members of the Medici family, Ippolito and Allesandro. When Rome fell and Clement became a virtual prisoner, the cardinal and the two young Medici men fled from Florence. The people took this opportunity to restore a republican form of government.

But Charles V was facing great pressure from other European rulers to accept responsibility for the brutal acts of his army in Rome. In response to this pressure, Charles made peace in June 1529 with Clement, who immediately began plans to regain control of Florence for the Medici family. Charles himself loaned Clement an army.

A Military Appointment

Florence had long been preparing for such a turn of events. Michelangelo, torn between loyalty to the Medici family and to his city, chose Florence. In 1527, he volunteered to help redesign and strengthen the city against the army all knew would come. By 1529, he had been placed in charge of the entire project, even though he had no experience in military architecture. His title was "governor and procurator general over the construction and fortification of the city walls and for other tasks relating to the defenses of the City of Florence."[87]

Michelangelo's designs, as de Tolnay wrote, "by their originality and ingenuity, marked a decisive turning point in the history of the architecture of fortification."[88] In fact, the designs were too original. The

Pope Clement VII flees as Charles V's army sacks Rome. The ravaging of the Eternal City marked the beginning of the end of the Renaissance.

signory, or city leaders, would not accept them. Furthermore, Michelangelo heard rumors that Florence's hired commander in chief, Maltesta Baglioni, was going to betray the city. Michelangelo found that guns had been placed where they would have little effect instead of where he had ordered.

Flight to Venice

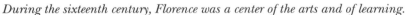

Michelangelo complained to the signory, but he was told that he was too suspicious. Angered and afraid of Baglioni's revenge, he left the city and went to Venice. He later wrote to a friend that "a certain person . . . whispered in my ear that, if I meant to save my life, I must not stay in Florence."[89] This may have been true, or it may have been another case of Michelangelo running from an imaginary danger. He returned to Florence in November at

the urging of friends. He was fined by the signory for having abandoned his responsibilities, but he was restored to his position as chief of the city's fortifications.

By this time, Clement's army had almost surrounded Florence. Michelangelo's fortifications were too strong to take by force, so it was decided to starve the city into surrender. Florence held out for ten months but finally gave up on August 3, 1530, betrayed by Baglioni, who switched sides when he saw the cause was lost. Clement treated the conquered city harshly, executing several leaders of the short-lived republic. Michelangelo stayed in hiding for weeks, but the pope needed him. Condivi wrote:

When the furor had subsided, Pope Clement wrote to Florence that Michelangelo was to be sought, and the pope's orders were that when he was found, if he were willing to continue the work he had already begun on the

During the sixteenth century, Florence was a center of the arts and of learning.

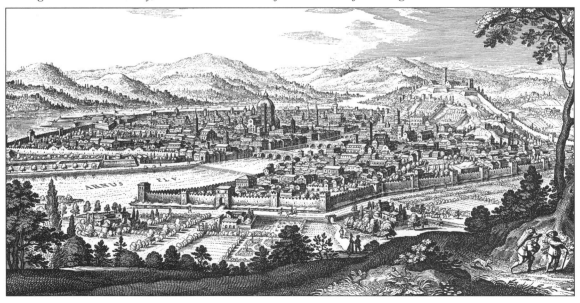

tombs, he should be treated with courtesy and allowed to go free. Learning of this, Michelangelo emerged and . . . he set about that project with such diligence that, impelled more by fear than by love, in a few months he made all those statues which appear in the sacristy of San Lorenzo. It is true that none of them have received the final touches; however they are all brought to such a stage that the excellence of the artist is very apparent, and the rough surfaces do not interfere with the perfection and the beauty of the work.[90]

Michelangelo had not completely neglected his art. His statue of *Victory*, intended for the Julius tomb, is thought to have been carved between 1527 and 1530. In the fall of 1530, however, he began working at a furious pace on the Medici chapel, the statues for the Medici tomb, and the Laurentian Library. He worked so hard that his health failed. His friend, Giovanni Mini, wrote to an acquaintance in Rome:

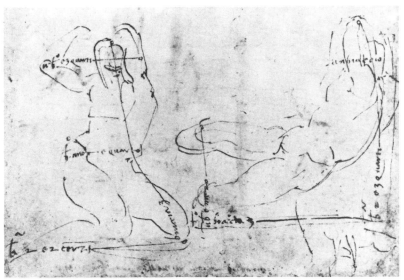

While the pope and kings battled each other, Michelangelo sculpted the exquisite statue of Victory *(above) for Julius II's tomb. In late 1530, he began work on numerous statues to adorn the Medici family chapel, tomb, and library. The sketches (left) are from these works.*

Michelangelo is not long for this life, unless measures for his welfare are taken. He is working very hard, eats little and poorly and sleeps even less. He is suffering from two ailments, in the head and in the heart. Neither is incurable, since he has a strong constitution. As for his head, Our Lord the Pope should give him dispensation from working in the sacristy [San Lorenzo] in the winter, the air there being bad for him. As for his heart, the best remedy would be if His Holiness succeeded in putting in order the matter [the Julius tomb] with the Duke of Urbino.[91]

In November 1531, the pope threatened Michelangelo with excommunication if he did not take care of himself and put aside all but the most important projects. He also continued to help Michelangelo in his long battle with Julius's heirs. Clement negotiated a new contract with the della Rovere family, and it was signed in April 1532. This even-smaller tomb was to be done in three years. Six statues were to be carved by Michelangelo, the rest by others. All costs were to be paid by Michelangelo from the money already paid to him by the della Rovere family. None of this actually took place, however. Instead, Michelangelo continued to work on the Medici chapel and library.

Sadness and Disappointments

The years from 1530 to 1534, although filled with work, were unhappy ones for Michelangelo. His favorite brother, Buonarroto, had died in 1527. His father died in 1531. Michelangelo was in poor health and felt guilty for not fulfilling the contract for

Allesandro de' Medici became duke of Florence in 1530. His murderous hatred for Michelangelo drove the artist from Florence.

the Julius tomb. For years, he had considered himself an old man and thought more and more about death. In 1530, although only fifty-five and at the height of his creativity, Michelangelo wrote:

> Ah, me! Ah, me! when thinking of the years,
> The vanished years, alas, I do not find
> Among them all one day that was my own!
> Fallacious hopes, desires of the unknown,
> Lamenting, loving, burning, and in tears
> (For human passions all have stirred my mind),
> Have held me, now I feel and know, confined

Both from the true and good still far
  away.
I perish day by day;
The sunshine fails, the shadows grow
  more dreary,
And I am near to fall, infirm and
  weary.[92]

These years were not happy ones for Florence either. Allesandro de' Medici, rumored to be the illegitimate son of Pope Clement, was formally made duke. Even as a boy, Allesandro had been cruel and moody, and the people of Florence dreaded his rule. He knew this, and he hated them in return. He especially hated Michelangelo, for reasons never made clear, and Michelangelo feared him. "There is no doubt," Condivi wrote, "that but for the pope's protection, he [Michelangelo] would have been removed from this world."[93] When Clement's health began to fail in the spring of 1534, Michelangelo made one last flight. He abruptly left San Lorenzo, the tomb, and the library and

went to Rome. For once, his fears and the danger were real. He arrived in Rome on September 23. Two days later, Pope Clement died. Michelangelo, now fifty-nine, never saw Florence again.

A Productive Period

Michelangelo's work from 1520 to 1534, although constantly interrupted by politics, war, and illness, produced some of his most important pieces. These include the four Florentine slaves, the *Victory*, the Laurentian Library, the Medici chapel, and the seven statues inside the chapel—the *capitani* (Giuliano and Lorenzo), the figures *Night*, *Day*, *Dusk*, and *Dawn*, and a Madonna.

The two buildings—the chapel and library—cannot be considered separately from the sculpture. Indeed, the chapel and the statues inside were designed as a single work. Instead of merely building a smaller duplicate of Brunelleschi's San

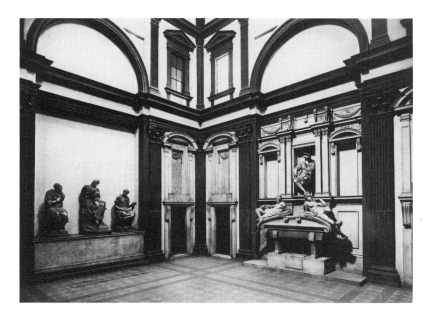

Michelangelo's statues adorn Lorenzo's tomb in the Medici chapel in Florence. The chapel's statues are among his most important works.

Symphony in Stone

The sculptures Michelangelo carved for the Medici tomb produced a powerful impact because they were presented as a group. John Addington Symonds described his reaction upon viewing this group.

"Standing before these statues, we do not cry, How beautiful! We murmur, How terrible, how grand! Yet, after long gazing, we find them gifted with beauty beyond grace. In each of them there is a palpitating thought, torn from the artist's soul and crystalized in marble. It has been said that architecture is petrified music. In the Sacristy of San Lorenzo we feel impelled to remember phrases of Beethoven. Each of these statues becomes for us a passion, fit for musical expression, but turned like Niobe to stone. They have the intellectual vagueness, the emotional certainty, that belong to the motives of a symphony. In their allegories, left without a key, sculpture has passed beyond her old domain of placid concrete form. The anguish of intolerable emotions, the quickening of the consciousness to a sense of suffering, the acceptance of the inevitable, the strife of the soul with destiny, the burden and the passion of mankind—that is what they contain in their cold chisel-tortured marble."

Lorenzo dome, Michelangelo added a mezzanine with windows to let in light. For the first time, he "was able to fit the surrounding space to his figures so that each was in keeping with the other. Now he succeeded in what he had failed to do with his *David*, his *Pietà* and his *Moses*—to utilize the light and space as he pleased, and he did so to great effect."[94]

Michelangelo paid as little attention to the established rules of architecture as he had to the rules of sculpture and painting. He took the usual columns, arches, and moldings and created an entirely new style. "This expression," Howard Hibbard wrote, "we learn here for the first time, was not to be suppressed by the traditional, mechanical demands of architecture: Michelangelo always refused to be satisfied with a routine traditional form."[95] This was also recognized at the time. Vasari wrote that the chapel was "extremely novel, and in [it] he departed a great deal from the kind of architecture regulated by proportion, order, and rule that other artists did according to common usage . . . but from which Michelangelo wanted to break away."[96]

The Laurentian Library

The chief feature of the Laurentian Library is the staircase leading to the reading room. It was built from Michelangelo's

(Above) The staircase to the Laurentian Library of the Medicis seems to cascade from the entrance, while the interior design (left) makes the room appear almost endless. These creations were the first in which Michelangelo was allowed to design not only the statuary but the space and architecture that formed their context.

original design in 1558, long after he left Florence. He envisioned the staircase as a stack of flat, oval boxes, each slightly smaller than the one below. It looks something like a series of short waterfalls. It is more a piece of sculpture than a staircase. Michelangelo "almost single-handed, invented the use of the interior stair as a ma-jor, sculptural feature of architectural de-sign."[97] It would be copied a century later by the architects of the Baroque period.

The statues vary from the very finished (the *capitani*) to the barely roughed out (the Florentine slaves). All, however, carry forward the idea of the *Dying Slave* and *Rebellious Slave*. They are not portrayals of

An idealized statue of Lorenzo sits above his tomb as if transcending the cares of the world of time depicted by the figures of Dawn *(right) and* Dusk.

people. Even the *capitani* are not modeled on the likenesses of the young Giuliano and Lorenzo. Instead, these statues represent emotions. *Night, Day, Dusk,* and *Dawn,* who lie under the *capitani,* are not grieving for Giuliano and Lorenzo. They reflect Michelangelo's own sorrow. Georg Brandes wrote:

> They are tired unto death, utterly sickened by life. There is no peace within them. They do not trouble to conceal their contempt of man. For them no joy in awakening to another day, no zest at high noon, no sweet repose in sleep. One thing they have in common—they suffer. They are the true children of Michelangelo, of the artist who never portrayed happiness. . . . For in the last reckoning these figures do not represent Day or Night—or indeed, anything to which a name can be given. What they reflect is the interior of Michelangelo's mind as it looked in the years from 1524 to 1534, made visible in perfect form.[98]

Michelangelo's Artistic Contribution

Michelangelo had shown the artists of his time that a work did not have to be a polished copy of the human form. He showed

Michelangelo's madonna in the Medici chapel has less detail than the earlier Pietà, *yet expresses an even deeper sorrow.*

details would lead, over time, to what is known as abstract art. Such artists as Pablo Picasso, whose figures are sometimes barely recognizable as human beings, owe much to Michelangelo's daring break from traditional art forms.

This was Michelangelo's greatest contribution to art. Certainly, he influenced many individual artists, such as Raphael, and his work led to entire movements in art, such as Mannerism and the Baroque. More important, however, is that he broke the established rules. He experimented and attempted new ways of expressing himself. He was so successful and famous that all artists, from then to now, have been more free to be bold and to go in new directions. As Vasari wrote:

> The license he allowed himself has served as a great encouragement to others to follow his example; and subsequently we have seen the creation of new kinds of fantastic ornamentation containing more of the grotesque than of rule or reason. . . . All artists are under a great and permanent obligation to Michelangelo, seeing that he broke the bonds and chains that had previously confined them to the creation of traditional forms.[99]

that the spirit of the work, and of the artist, could be captured with fewer details. The face of Mary in the Medici madonna is plain and angular compared to that of the *Pietà*. The texture is rough. The marks of chisels can be seen. Yet it conveys more sorrow. This idea of expressing more emotion with fewer and fewer

7 Friends and Religion

The years after Michelangelo's permanent move from Florence to Rome were probably his happiest since he had left Lorenzo de' Medici's palace in 1492. He was safe from Allesandro's hostility. He could resume work on the Julius tomb. Most important, he began to form strong, lifelong friendships.

Michelangelo was not, as some have written, a man "scarcely feeling the need for friends"[100] who kept people at a distance. He had simply been too busy. Coughlan wrote that "in his blackest moods he was, to put it plainly, impossible. . . . Yet he somehow stirred the protective instinct in people; they wanted to take care of him. . . . For a great many years Michelangelo's commitments to friendship had been limited by his obsessive commitment to his art."[101]

Michelangelo already had such a good friend in Rome that it was perhaps his strongest reason for remaining there. In 1532, he had met a young, Roman nobleman named Tommaso de Cavalieri, and the two formed a strong friendship. Indeed, Michelangelo "certainly, in some sense, fell violently in love."[102] Cavalieri remained Michelangelo's friend for life, tending to him in his final illness many years later.

This relationship was more important to Michelangelo's poetry than to his art. He did some drawings for Cavalieri, as he sometimes did for good friends, but it is the love poems he wrote to the young man that are some of the finest of the Renaissance. It was not considered inappropriate at this time for men to express strong feelings of friendship and admiration for one another as "love." Michelangelo could freely write to Cavalieri that "I

Michelangelo as painted by his biographer and contemporary Giorgio Vasari.

Voluntary Exile

Not even the promise of honors from the duke of Florence could entice Michelangelo to return there from Rome after 1534. In his autobiography, Benvenuto Cellini described one attempt.

"Before I left for Rome, I showed it [a letter from Michelangelo] to the Duke [Cosimo of Florence], who read it with much kindly interest, and said to me: 'Benvenuto, if you write to him, and can persuade him to return to Florence, I will make him a member of the Forty-Eight [the Florentine senate].' Accordingly, I wrote a letter full of warmth, and offered in the Duke's name a hundred times more than my commission carried; but not wanting to make any mistake, I showed this to the Duke before I sealed it, saying to his most illustrious Excellency: 'Prince, perhaps I have made him too many promises.' He replied: 'Michelangelo deserves more than you have promised, and I will bestow on him still greater favors.' To this letter he [Michelangelo] sent no answer, and I could see that the Duke was much offended with him. . . . Then I went to visit Michelangelo Buonarroti, and repeated what I had written from Florence to him in the Duke's name. He replied that he was engaged upon the fabric of St. Peter's, and that this would prevent him from leaving Rome. . . . I added much about future favors, in the form of a message from the Duke. Upon this he looked me hard in the face, and said with a sarcastic smile: 'And you! To what extent are you satisfied with him [Duke Cosimo]?' Although I replied that I was extremely contented and was very well treated by his Excellency, he showed that he was acquainted with the greater part of my annoyances, and gave us his."

had made you certain of the very great, nay, measureless love I bear you . . . I could as easily forget your name as the food by which I live. Nay, it were easier to forget the food, which only nourishes my body miserably, than your name, which nourishes both body and soul."[103]

Michelangelo and Cavalieri

When the Roman Catholic church later became more conservative in response to the Protestant movement, attitudes toward expressions of friendship between men changed. Michelangelo's grandnephew, who published the first edition of the artist's poems, changed "he" to "she" and "him" to "her" to make it appear as if they had been written to a woman. In 1549, a man named Pietro Aretino started rumors that Michelangelo and Cavalieri were lovers and not just friends. Aretino tried to blackmail Michelangelo by offering to quiet the rumors in exchange for some drawings. Michelangelo refused.

There is no evidence that Michelangelo had anything but deep and lasting friendships with men. The artist himself rebuked those who suspected love affairs:

> For faithful guide unto my laboring
> heart
> Beauty was given me at birth,
> To be my glass [mirror] and lamp in
> either art.
> Who thinketh otherwise misknows her
> worth,
> For highest beauty only gives me light
> To carve and paint aright.
> Rash is the thought and vain
> That maketh beauty from the senses
> grow.[104]

Vittoria Colonna

Michelangelo had many other friends in Rome, including artists, writers, and churchmen. The most important, however, was Vittoria Colonna. She was the only woman known to have ever influenced him.

After the death of her husband, the marquis of Pescara, in 1525, Vittoria turned to religion and lived mostly in seclusion. She began to write that the Roman Catholic church had moved away from the teachings of Jesus. She wanted a return to basic, fundamental Christianity. She believed that people's souls could be saved only through their faith, not through good deeds on earth and not through the rituals of the church. She became part of a group of religious thinkers who produced the Italian Reformation.

Vittoria and Michelangelo met in 1536, and the artist was soon writing poetry to her. He was not in love, and the poems, in fact, are less romantic than those written to Cavalieri. Their friendship, although passionate, was intellectual rather than physical. Michelangelo began to turn away from his Neoplatonic, half-Christian, half-pagan view of religion. He worried about the salvation of his soul and believed Vittoria had shown him the way to God. He wrote to her:

> A man, a god rather, inside a woman,
> Through her mouth has his speech.
> And this has made me such
> I'll never again be mine after I listen.
> Ever since she has stolen
> Me from myself, I'm sure.
> Outside myself I'll give myself my pity.
> Her beautiful features summon
> Upward from false desire.
> So that I see death in all other beauty.
> You who bring souls, O lady,
> Through fire and water to felicity,
> See to it I do not return to me.[105]

Two New Works Emphasize Religious Themes

Michelangelo's religious conversion had an enormous influence on his art. Although the human body remained the focus of his work, his themes were Christian

Michelangelo began painting The Last Judgment *on the eastern wall of the Sistine Chapel twenty-four years after finishing the ceiling frescoes.*

and dealt mostly with death and salvation.

Since the death of Pope Clement in 1534, Michelangelo had been working on the Julius tomb. He would have liked to have been left alone to finish this project, now almost thirty years old, but the new pope, Paul III, wanted his services. In 1535, he named Michelangelo director of painting, sculpture, and architecture for the Vatican. When Michelangelo protested, Paul came to his workshop with a group of cardinals. One of the cardinals, seeing the *Moses*, exclaimed, "This statue alone is sufficient to do honor to the tomb of Pope Julius."[106] The pope then told Michelangelo he would arrange for the della Rovere family to accept the *Moses*, two other statues by Michelangelo, and three from some other sculptor.

Paul wanted Michelangelo to return to the Sistine Chapel to do two fresco paintings, *The Last Judgment* for the altar wall and *The Fall of the Rebel Angels* (which was never begun) for the entrance wall. *The Last Judgment* had actually been suggested by Pope Clement in 1532, and Michelangelo had already done some preliminary cartoons. He began the fresco in 1536, about the time of his religious conversion by Vittoria Colonna. She had once written, "Christ comes twice: the first time . . . he only shows his great kindness, his clemency and his pity. The second time he comes armed and shows his justice, his majesty, his grandeur, his almighty power, and there is no longer any time for pity or room for pardon."[107] This is the Christ Michelangelo depicted in *The Last Judgment*.

It was a dramatic change for Michelangelo, both in subject matter and in artistic style. The Renaissance faith in human ability, which Michelangelo showed so well in the *David*, is gone. The sinners in *The Last Judgment*, no matter how they struggle, cannot escape their fate. As Mary and the saints look helplessly on, these sinners are condemned by a merciless Christ and are driven into hell by demons. The feeling is one of gloom and depression. When Pope Paul saw it unveiled in 1541, he fell to his knees, calling on God to forgive him for his sins. *The Last Judgment* has been called "the image in which Michelangelo's own *terribilitá* conjoins absolutely with the meaning and the stature of the theme, and it is his most awesome creation."[108] Artists came from throughout Europe to see and sketch it. It set the tone for religious painting for the next century and was "a remarkable expression of the fundamental doctrine of the Italian Reformation."[109]

The Last Judgment has been called "a turning point in Michelangelo's artistic style . . . and to a substantial degree in the style of the *cinquecento* [1500s]."[110] Instead of large, grand figures, as on the Sistine ceiling, the scene is crammed full of twisting, agitated bodies. The movement is swirling and circular. The dead rise up from the left, Christ dominates the center, and the damned fall into hell on the right. "In all of its complexities, *The Last Judgment* sounded a knell for the calm classicism of High Renaissance art and signaled the coming triumph of its stormy successor style, Mannerism."[111]

The painting of *The Last Judgment* was not without humorous moments. One of the pope's officials, Biagio da Cesena, who

Christ is a stern judge in Michelangelo's Last Judgment. *The figure reflects the influence of the Reformation on the aging artist and his concern for his own salvation.*

Michelangelo's painting of The Crucifixion of St. Peter, *done for the Vatican's Pauline Chapel, was one of the artist's last works.*

saw the work before it was finished, complained about the nude figures. Michelangelo replied by giving Biagio's features to a horned devil. When Biagio complained to the pope, Paul joked, "Had the painter sent you to purgatory [halfway between earth and hell], I would use my best efforts to get you released; but I exercise no influence in Hell; there you are beyond redemption."[112] In another place, Saint Bartholomew (who was skinned alive) is shown in heaven, holding his old skin, which bears the tired, worn-out features of Michelangelo himself.

Fifteen years after it was finished, another pope, Paul IV, objected to the nudity and wanted the entire work destroyed. He was persuaded, instead, to have veils and drapes painted over the offending portions. "Tell the pope that this is a trivial matter, and can be easily arranged," Michelangelo wrote. "Let him set to straightening out the world, for pictures are quickly straightened out."[113] Daniele da Volterra, one of Michelangelo's assistants, was given the job and thereafter was known as *Il Braghettone*, the britches maker.

Pope Paul soon had another task for Michelangelo. He wanted the artist to paint two frescoes in the new Pauline Chapel of the Vatican. One was to be *The Crucifixion of St. Peter* and the other *The Conversion of St. Paul.* They were to be Michelangelo's last paintings. The first was done from 1542 to 1545 and the second from 1545 to 1550. Like *The Last Judgment*, they are highly religious but display little of the passion of earlier works. Howard Hibbard wrote that Michelangelo "seems to have put his art solely at the service of faith."[114]

Later, the artist himself was to write:

> There's no painting or sculpture now
>   that quiets
> The soul that's pointed toward that
>   whole Love
> That on the cross opened Its arms to
>   take us.[115]

The Julius Tomb Is Finished

During the three years Michelangelo worked on *The Crucifixion of St. Peter,* he finally brought one of the most painful chapters of his life to an end. He finished the Julius tomb. He decided that the *Rebellious Slave* and the *Dying Slave* were too large and bulky for the final version of the tomb. Instead, he carved two women from the Bible, Rachel and Leah. These statues, "which display stretches of bland, inexpressive carving,"[116] in no way equal his earlier works. They stand on either side of the *Moses* in the tomb that was finally unveiled in 1545, forty years after it was begun. Michelangelo was not proud of this final version. Neither was the della Rovere family. Julius's body was never moved to the tomb. The coffin on top remains empty to this day.

Michelangelo finished the tomb of Pope Julius II forty years after he started work on it. Despite the grandeur of the Moses *at the base, the late pope's family was dissatisfied with the finished work and did not inter Julius's body there.*

To Vittoria Colonna

In this poem taken from Michelangelo: A Self-Portrait, *Michelangelo expresses his grief over the death of Vittoria Colonna, the only woman with whom he ever formed a friendship.*

"When the prime mover of my many sighs
Heaven took through death from out her earthy place,
Nature, that never made so fair a face,
Remained ashamed, and tears were in all eyes.
O fate, unheeding my impassioned cries!
O hopes fallacious! O thou spirit of grace,
Where art thou now? Earth holds in its embrace
Thy lovely limbs, thy holy thoughts the skies.
Vainly did cruel death attempt to stay
The rumor of thy virtuous renown,
        That Lethe's waters could not
            wash away!
    A thousand leaves since he hath
            stricken thee down,
    Speak of thee, nor to thee could
            Heaven convey,
    Except through death, a refuge
            and a crown."

Vittoria Colonna was a close friend of Michelangelo.

Difficult Years

These were difficult years physically for Michelangelo, even though he had found spiritual peace. In 1540, while painting *The Last Judgment*, he fell from the scaffolding and could not work again for months. He became seriously ill in 1544. He complained to Vasari that "painting, especially in fresco, is not work for an old man."[117] He became depressed by the death of Vittoria Colonna in 1547. He was now almost seventy-five years old, and he thought nothing awaited him except death. He wrote:

> Here I am, poor and alone
> Enclosed like the pith in its rind,
> Or like a spirit holed up in a decanter
>   [bottle];
> And my dark tomb affords little
>   flight . . . .
> My loins are strained, I'm out of
>   breath,
> Fractured and broken by my labor,
>   and death
> Is the hostel [inn] where I eat and live
>   on credit.
> Melancholy is my joy and my repose
> And these discomforts; for to him who
>   seeks it
> God will give calamity! . . .
> What avails it to try to create so many
>   childish things
> If they've but brought me to this end,
>   like one
> Who crosses o'er the sea and then
>   drowns on the strand.
> Precious art, in which for a while I en-
>   joyed such renown,
> Has left me in this state:
> Poor, old, and a slave in others' power.
> I am undone if I do not die soon.[118]

As usual, Michelangelo exaggerated. He was still fairly healthy for a man of his age. He was not poor. Indeed, he was rich by the standards of the time, although he never spent much on himself. And rather than a "slave in others' power," he was per-haps the most respected and admired man in Europe. The king of France wrote to him and begged for any work of art, however small. Pope Paul III said that he would gladly "give up some of his years and some of his own blood to add to Michelangelo's life."[119] Charles de Tolnay wrote, "Everyone imitated him in style. . . . From 1540 onwards, European art be-comes Michelangelesque."[120]

Michelangelo's most important contri-bution to future artists, in addition to giv-ing them the freedom to experiment, was to give them a new and more respectable position in society. He "had achieved sta-tus and riches unknown to previous artists. . . . [His] dignity, increased by his own accomplishment and manner, helped raise the station of artists to a level they had never before enjoyed."[121] The great masters of the sixteenth and seventeenth centuries, living in splendor, owed much to Michelangelo. He was the "artist-philosopher, the artist-poet, an aristocrat of the spirit."[122]

The end of his life, longed for by Michelangelo, was still a long way off. His body was weakening, but his creative spirit still burned. Pope Paul saw this and, in 1547, appointed him chief architect of Saint Peter's Church. Michelangelo pro-tested, as usual, that "architecture is not my trade."[123] Paul stood firm, and Saint Pe-ter's proved to be Michelangelo's most en-during monument.

8 Michelangelo the Architect

Michelangelo's experience in architecture as of 1545 was slight. The Laurentian Library would not be completed for another ten years. He had begun his design for the Piazza del Campdoglio, Rome's principal public place, but it was not built until after his death. Only the Medici chapel in Florence, finished from his plans after he left

Pope Paul III hired Michelangelo to finish Saint Peter's Church after the Vatican architect, Sangallo, died in 1546.

the city in 1532, had actually been completed.

Yet when Pope Paul III became unhappy with Antonio da Sangallo's design of the cornice, the decorative molding around the top, of his family palace, the Palazzo Farnese, he asked the sixty-year-old Michelangelo for his opinion. Michelangelo wrote that Sangallo's design had "no orderly disposition at all. . . . Here rather everything within is disorder. . . . This cornice displays more readily barbarous or other qualities."[124] The pope asked Rome's leading architects to submit plans for the cornice. He chose Michelangelo's. Sangallo, greatly humiliated and embittered, died the following year.

Sangallo had also been for thirty years the chief architect of Saint Peter's Church. Upon Sangallo's death, the pope gave the task to Michelangelo. Michelangelo "firmly refused the position, alleging that it was not his art; and he refused it in such a way that the pope was compelled to order him to take it."[125] One of Michelangelo's conditions for accepting the position was that he would receive no pay; he wished to work only for the glory of God.

Saint Peter's dates back to about the year 330 when a church was built on Vatican Hill over the traditional site of the tomb of Saint Peter. The church became

Antonio da Sangallo was the chief architect of Saint Peter's for thirty years.

one of the centers of Christianity. It was the church of the popes. Kings and emperors, including Charlemagne in 800, came to Saint Peter's to be crowned.

By the fifteenth century, the old church was in danger of collapse. Rebuilding was begun in the mid-1400s but halted in 1455. It was begun again in 1505 by Pope Julius II, and Michelangelo himself was the cause. His original design for Julius's tomb was so massive that the pope decided that only a new Saint Peter's could hold it.

Michelangelo's enemy Bramante was chosen as architect. After Bramante's death in 1515, the work was continued by others, including Raphael, Michelangelo's friend Giuliano da Sangallo, and Giuliano's nephew Antonio da Sangallo. Progress was slow. Popes and architects

came and went so frequently that by 1546, the final shape of the church had not been decided.

Bramante's design had been a Greek cross, one with arms of equal length. Sangallo had changed it to a Latin cross, with the bottom arm longer than the other three. Even though Bramante had been his enemy, Michelangelo knew his plan was better. After inspecting Sangallo's model, Michelangelo wrote:

> It cannot be denied that Bramante was as worthy an architect as any since ancient times. He made the first plan of St. Peter's, not full of confusion, but clear and simple, full of light and entirely free-standing, in such a way that no damage was done to the palace and it was considered a beautiful thing, as is still evident; so that whoever departs from this order of Bramante, as Sangallo has done, has departed from the truth; and that this is so, anyone with dispassionate eyes can see in his model. With that circle which he puts outside, he first cuts off all the light from Bramante's plan; and not only that, but in itself it has no light at all.[126]

Michelangelo Takes Up the Rebuilding

Sangallo was dead, but many people, including cardinals, his assistants, and those who supplied materials, wanted to see Sangallo's plan used. When Michelangelo began dismissing assistants and canceling contracts, the members of this "sect of Sangallo"[127] decided to get rid of him. The so-called Sangallists kept up a steady stream of complaints to the pope, accusing Michelangelo of everything from incompetence to theft.

The pope finally issued what has been called the "diploma of Paul." In it, the pope acknowledged Michelangelo as "a member of our household and our regular dining-companion." He confirmed his approval of Michelangelo's design and appointed him chief architect of Saint Peter's for life. He also gave Michelangelo "authority to change, re-fashion, enlarge, and contract the . . . building as shall seem best to him . . . without seeking permission . . . from anyone else whatsoever."[128]

This appointment would be confirmed by three more popes, but it still did not stop the Sangallists. In 1551, after Paul III's death, they persuaded the new pope, Julius III, to convene a meeting in Saint Peter's. There, a Sangallist cardinal, Marcello Cervini, charged that Michelangelo's

A statue of Pope Julius III, Michelangelo's friend and advocate.

design would not allow enough light into the church. According to Vasari:

> Michelangelo said: "Monsignor, three more windows of travertine [a kind of stone] are to go to the vaulting." "You never told us that," said the cardinal. "I am not obliged to tell you or anybody else what I propose to do," retorted the artist. "Your office [task] is to collect the money, and protect it from thieves; you must leave the design and charge of the building to me." Turning to the pope, he said, "Holy Father, you see what profit I have; for if these labors do not benefit my soul, I am losing my time and trouble." The pope, who loved him, laid his hands on his shoulders, and said: "Do not doubt that you will gain both in soul and body."[129]

Julius then ended the meeting by inviting Michelangelo to dine with him the next day so that they might discuss the work on Saint Peter's.

The Sangallists never gave up. Their numbers grew during the years as Michelangelo, always a difficult person to work with, continued to make enemies. His letters complained of untrustworthy workers, inferior materials, and plots against his life. In 1557, Michelangelo wrote that he could not go to Florence because "I should give satisfaction to sundry robbers here, and should bring ruin upon" the building.[130] In 1560, he asked to be dismissed "as perhaps my self-interest or my old age deceive me, and I may be doing injury to the building.[131]

Yet construction continued. Michelangelo tore down some of what Sangallo had built and simplified Bramante's plan, making the church less crowded and let-

ting in more light. He thought of the building as he would a piece of sculpture, a single unit instead of a collection of parts. In fact, he considered a building to be almost a living thing. He once wrote, "The members of an architectural structure follow the laws exemplified in the human body. He who . . . is not a good master of the nude . . . cannot understand the principles of architecture."[132]

Saint Peter's was completed long after Michelangelo's death. The architects who came after him made many changes. Since Michelangelo left no detailed plans, it is impossible to know how much of the outer design is his. He did, however, leave a model for the magnificent dome. The dome of Saint Peter's is considered one of the world's greatest works, and it placed Michelangelo among the world's greatest architects.

Michelangelo had grown up in the shadow of Brunelleschi's dome of the

(Top) The interior of Saint Peter's was conceived as a single unit by Michelangelo. (Right) Michelangelo's drawing of the exterior of Saint Peter's. The dome, inspired by that of the Florence cathedral, is considered an architectural masterpiece.

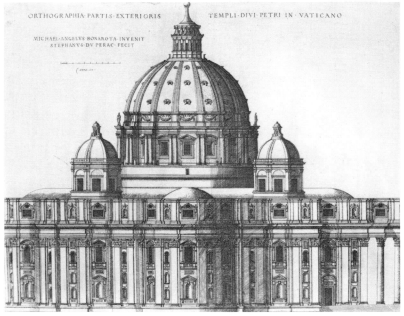

cathedral in Florence, and he used it as a model for Saint Peter's dome. He wrote to his nephew in Florence asking for the exact dimensions. He designed the dome as a hemisphere with a tall lantern tower on top. It was finally finished in 1590, only slightly altered from the original design. Called by one critic "the greatest ever built"[133] and by another an "inspiration of creative fantasy,"[134] Saint Peter's dome has influenced architects ever since. Christopher Wren used it as a model for the dome of Saint Paul's Cathedral in London. The dome of the Capitol in Washington, D.C., and those of many state capitols owe their existence to Michelangelo.

Michelangelo's Contribution to Architecture

Michelangelo's architectural projects, though few, revolutionized the art. He was concerned not as much with constructing a building as with molding the space inside it using light and shadow. His buildings were neither monuments in themselves, as in ancient architecture, nor the "envelopes for man"[135] of the Renaissance. Michelangelo showed future architects how to combine grandeur and functionalism. One biographer wrote:

The finished Saint Peter's, including the later additions of a façade by Maderno and a piazza surrounded by columns by Bernini.

Preferring Solitude

Michelangelo had many more friends in later life than as a young man. Still, he preferred to be alone with his thoughts than to pretend in the company of others, as this poem of his shows. It is taken from Michelangelo: A Self-Portrait.

"Ill hath he chosen his part who seeks to please
The worthless world—ill hath he chosen his part,
For often must he wear the look of ease
When grief is at his heart;
And often in his hours of happy feeling
With sorrow must his countenance be hung,
And ever his own better thoughts concealing
Must he in stupid grandeur's praise be loud,
And to the errors of the ignorant crowd
Assent with lying tongue.
Thus much would I conceal that none should know
What secret cause I have for silent woe;
And taught by many a melancholy proof
That those whom fortune favors it pollutes,
I from the blind and faithless world aloof,
Nor fear its envy nor desire its praise,
But choose my path through solitary ways."

Architecture became Michelangelo's chief old-age means of expression. Architectural design aroused none of the unconscious anxieties that so frustrated his later sculptural projects, and the abstract repertory [variety] of architectural forms became personal and sculptural in his hands. He changed Renaissance architecture in larger ways as well; what had been an organization of parts . . . became sculptural, organic wholes. This achievement was not finally appreciated until the following century, when Borromini, taking Michelangelo as an inspiration, produced the greatest expression of the style we call Baroque. Michelangelo became in the end not merely a designer of genius . . . but a God-like molder of space and mass.[136]

Although architecture occupied most of his time, Michelangelo remained at heart a sculptor. Sometime in the late 1540s, he began working for his own pleasure on *The Deposition of Christ.* He carved at night, using a candle mounted on a paper cap as a light. The work shows Jesus, taken down from the cross, supported by Mary, Nicodemus, and Mary Magdalene. Michelangelo intended the statue to go above his own tomb, he told Condivi, and made Nicodemus both a physical and spiritual self-portrait. "His old, sad face, surrounded by the heavy cowl [hood]," wrote John Addington Symonds, "looks down

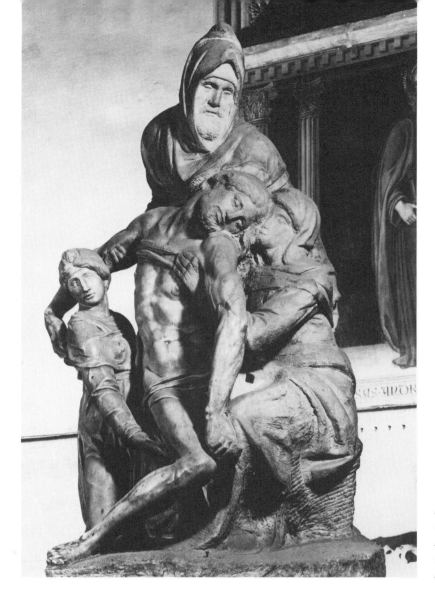

In his Deposition of Christ, *also known as the Florence Pietà, Michelangelo carved his own face on the figure of Nicodemus (top).*

forever with a tenderness beyond expression, repeating mutely through the years how much of anguish and of blood divine the redemption of man's soul hath cost."[137]

The *Deposition* was almost lost. In 1555, Michelangelo, who even in old age carved with "impetuosity and fury,"[138] accidentally knocked a piece off Mary's arm. Angry, most likely at himself and the loss of his abilities, he broke the statue into pieces until his servant stopped him. The pieces

were later put together and finished, with Michelangelo's permission, by another sculptor, Tiberio Calcagni. The statue now stands in the cathedral in Florence instead of above Michelangelo's tomb.

Michelangelo's health was failing, but his mind remained alert. He had many friends and displayed flashes of humor seldom seen in his younger days. Once, when asked his opinion of a portrait, he gave the standard compliment—that it

Michelangelo Summarized

John Addington Symonds ended his biography of Michelangelo with this view of the artist's life and career.

"At the end, then, a sound critic returns to think of Michelangelo . . . as tradition and the total tenor of his life display him to our admiration. Incalculable, incomprehensible, incommensurable: yes, all souls, the least and greatest, attack them as we will, are that. But definitely in solitary sublimity, like a supreme mountain seen from a vast distance, soaring over shadowy hills and misty plains into the clear ether of immortal fame. Viewed thus, he lives forever as the type and symbol of a man, much-suffering, continually laboring, gifted with keen but rarely indulged passions, whose energies from boyhood to extreme old age were dedicated with unswerving purpose to the service of one master, plastic [sculpting] art. On his deathbed he may have felt, like [poet Robert] Browning, in that sweetest of his poems, 'other heights in other lives, God willing.' But for this earthly pilgrimage, he was contented to leave the example of a noble nature made perfect and completed in itself by addition to one commanding impulse. We cannot cite another hero of the modern world who more fully and with greater intensity realized the main end of human life, which is self-effectuation, self-realization, self-manifestation in one of the many lines of labor to which men may be called and chosen. Had we more of such individuals, the symphony of civilization would be infinitely glorious."

Michelangelo embodied the spirit of the Renaissance.

looked as if it were about to speak. When someone asked what the portrait would say, Michelangelo replied, "That not a single part in it is any good."[139] Another time, when someone told him he had "the brain of a Jove," Michelangelo answered, "But it takes the hammer of Vulcan to get anything out of it."[140]

Michelangelo's illnesses became more frequent, yet he was still able at age eighty-five to inspect the work on Saint Peter's on horseback. He went for walks in all kinds of weather. Eventually, however, his hand became too unsteady to draw even a straight line. By 1563, his writing was so poor that he could only sign the letters he had dictated to others. At the request of Duke Cosimo de' Medici, who had often tried to get Michelangelo to return to Florence, the artist's house was watched to prevent drawings or other works from being stolen after his death.

On February 12, 1564, Michelangelo was still carving away, if feebly, on another statue. Two days later, however, Calcagni went to see him. He found the artist walking aimlessly in the rain. "What would you have me do?" he asked Calcagni. "I am ill and cannot find rest anywhere."[141] He was led back to his house and spent the next four days mostly in bed. Michelangelo knew death was near. His friends came one by one to say goodbye. Tommaso de Cavalieri sat with him for hours. In spite of all he had accomplished, Michelangelo felt his life was incomplete. "I regret that I have not done enough for the salvation of my soul," he said on his deathbed, "and that I am dying just as I am beginning to learn the alphabet of my profession."[142]

Michelangelo died late on the night of February 18, only a few weeks before his eighty-ninth birthday. He left a sizable amount of money to his nephew, Lionardo. Only three partially blocked-out statues and ten drawings were found in his house. Michelangelo had burned the rest, reluctant to let others see his unfinished work, even after his death.

The pope, Pius IV, wanted Michelangelo buried in Rome in Saint Peter's, but Duke Cosimo had other ideas. He had been unable to persuade the artist to return to Florence in life, but he was determined to bring him back in death. Michelangelo's body was secretly smuggled out of Rome, wrapped in canvas and concealed as merchandise.

In Florence, Michelangelo was given the kind of funeral usually reserved for kings and popes. An elaborate stand was made for the coffin by his fellow artists. Poems, songs, and speeches were composed and printed. The nobles and artists of Florence packed the church. Duke Cosimo donated the marble for a sculpture by Vasari for the tomb. Earlier, when Michelangelo's coffin had been carried to its final resting place at his neighborhood church of Santa Croce,

> all the painters, sculptors and architects met . . . bringing nothing but a velvet pall [cloth] with gold fringe to cover the coffin, on which lay a crucifix. At midnight they all stood about the body, the oldest and best artists supplying a quantity of torches, the younger men crowding to carry the bier, esteeming themselves happy if they could raise it on their shoulders, to be able to boast in after days of having borne the body of the greatest man their art had ever known.[143]

A Towering Genius

Anyone studying Michelangelo has an almost overwhelming number of sources. Although not as productive as some artists of his time mainly because of his refusal to use assistants, Michelangelo left numerous works, many more than described in this book. While some, like the *Battle of Cascina* cartoon, the satyr's head that attracted Lorenzo, and the sleeping cupid, have been lost, most of his works remain. Each generation of critics and art historians brings forth new, fresh interpretations of these masterpieces, now almost five hundred years old.

In addition to works, Michelangelo also left words. Hundreds of the letters and poems written over his long life have been preserved and translated. Scholars continue to read them in search of keys to understanding the man and his art. Some of his writings provide clues; others only make the mysteries deeper.

More has been written about Michelangelo than perhaps any other person in the history of art. As one biographer said simply, "The literature is vast."[144] Some artists gain renown only after their death, but Michelangelo was one of the most famous men of his century. At least two biographies of him were written during his lifetime, and dozens have been written since, to say nothing of the many volumes of interpretation of his works.

This wealth of material, however, can be a curse as well as a blessing. Since Michelangelo rarely analyzed his own art, this task has been left to others, and these interpretations vary greatly, sometimes contradicting one another. Interpretation of art is not an exact science and is, like beauty, mostly in the eye of the beholder. In his biography, John Addington

One of the hundreds of letters and poems left by Michelangelo.

The Sistine Chapel is still a worldwide tourist attraction and object of study.

Symonds called Michelangelo unknowable, but that has not stopped Symonds and others from trying to know him. Nor should it. Michelangelo's importance to art, from the sixteenth century through the twentieth, is too vast to fit neatly inside one critic's theory. Michelangelo's contributions and legacies will continue to be studied and uncovered.

All the questions and theories surrounding Michelangelo mean little to most of the millions of people who flock to the Sistine Chapel, the artist's house in Florence, or the Louvre in Paris to see his work. His paintings and statues are perhaps the best known and best loved in the world. One does not need a degree in art history to admire the power of the *David* or the tenderness of the *Pietà*. Tourists from Tokyo or Toledo may not fall to their knees before *The Last Judgment*, as Pope Paul did, but they may be similarly affected. And who is to say that a teenager's idea of the emotions expressed in *Night* and *Dawn* is less valid than a scholar's?

The world continues to learn more about Michelangelo, not only through study and interpretation but also from physical discoveries. The wooden crucifix he carved for the head of Santo Spirito was found only in 1961 and shows another aspect of his style. The Sistine Chapel ceiling underwent a thorough cleaning and is providing a clearer look at Michelangelo's technique and use of color.

Who knows what discoveries are yet to come? A similar restoration is planned for *The Last Judgment*, partially blackened in areas by centuries of smoke from altar candles. What will it show?

Michelangelo's works spoke to the people of the Renaissance. They speak just as clearly today and will continue to as long as the human spirit exists. Not everyone hears the same message, but none can deny the genius of the speaker.

House of Medici Family Tree

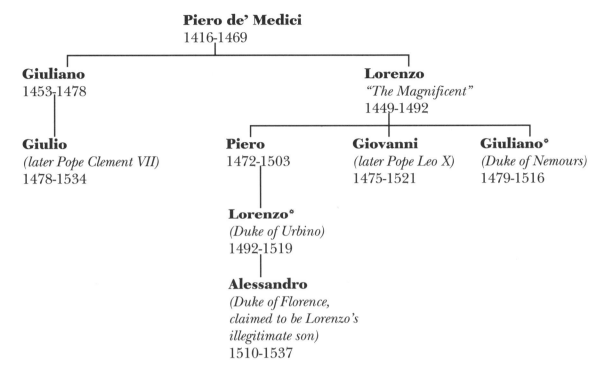

Piero de' Medici
1416-1469

Giuliano
1453-1478

Lorenzo
"The Magnificent"
1449-1492

Giulio
(later Pope Clement VII)
1478-1534

Piero
1472-1503

Giovanni
(later Pope Leo X)
1475-1521

Giuliano*
(Duke of Nemours)
1479-1516

Lorenzo*
(Duke of Urbino)
1492-1519

Alessandro
*(Duke of Florence,
claimed to be Lorenzo's
illegitimate son)*
1510-1537

* The "capitani" of Michelangelo's Medici tomb at San Lorenzo in Florence

Popes Under Whom Michelangelo Worked

Julius II
(Giuliano della Rovere)
1503-1513

Leo X
(Giovanni de' Medici)
1513-1521

Adrian VI
(Adrian Florensz)
1522-1523

Clement VII
(Giulio de' Medici)
1523-1534

Paul III
(Alessandro Farnese)
1534-1549

Julius III
*(Giovanni Maria Ciocchi
del Monte)*
1550-1555

Marcellus III
(Marcello Cervini)
1555 (Three weeks)

Paul IV
(Gian Pietro Carafa)
1555-1559

Pius IV
(Giovan Angelo de' Medici)
1559-1565

Notes

Chapter 1: An Early Talent

1. Robert Coughlan, *The World of Michelangelo: 1475-1564*. New York: Time-Life Books, 1966.
2. Ascanio Condivi, *The Life of Michelangelo*. Translated by Alice Sedgwick Wohl. Baton Rouge: Louisiana State University Press, 1976.
3. Giorgio Vasari, *The Lives of the Painters, Sculptors, and Architects*. Translated by A.B. Hinds. London: J.M. Dent & Sons, 1973.
4. Vasari, *The Lives of the Painters, Sculptors, and Architects*.
5. Howard Hibbard, *Michelangelo*. 2d ed. New York: Harper & Row, 1974.
6. Vasari, *The Lives of the Painters, Sculptors, and Architects*.
7. Condivi, *The Life of Michelangelo*.
8. Charles de Tolnay, *Michelangelo*. Translated by Gaynor Woodhouse. Princeton, NJ: Princeton University Press, 1975.
9. Vasari, *The Lives of the Painters, Sculptors, and Architects*.

Chapter 2: Entering the World of Art

10. Wallace K. Ferguson, *The Renaissance*. New York: Holt, Rinehart & Winston, 1940.
11. John R. Hale, *Renaissance*. New York: Time-Life Books, 1965.
12. Matteo Palmieri, quoted in Hale, *Renaissance*.
13. Richard L. DeMolen, *Meaning of the Renaissance and Reformation*. New York: Houghton Mifflin, 1974.
14. Gianozzo Manetti, quoted in Hale, *Renaissance*.
15. Beatrice Farwell, "Giotto di Bondone," in *Encyclopedia of Painting*. New York: Crown, 1979.
16. Leonardo da Vinci, *Treatise on Painting*. Translated by A. Philip McMahon. Princeton, NJ: Princeton University Press, 1956.
17. Coughlan, *The World of Michelangelo*.
18. Hale, *Renaissance*.

Chapter 3: Florence

19. de Tolnay, *Michelangelo*.
20. Michelangelo Buonarroti in *Michelangelo: A Self-Portrait*. Edited by Robert J. Clements. New York: New York University Press, 1968.
21. Vasari, *The Lives of the Painters, Sculptors, and Architects*.
22. Condivi, *The Life of Michelangelo*.
23. Condivi, *The Life of Michelangelo*.
24. Coughlan, *The World of Michelangelo*.
25. Condivi, *The Life of Michelangelo*.
26. Benvenuto Cellini, *The Autobiography*. Translated by John Addington Symonds. New York: Grolier, 1978.
27. Farwell, "Michelangelo Buonarroti," in *Encyclopedia of Painting*.
28. Condivi, *The Life of Michelangelo*.

Chapter 4: A Great Sculptor

29. Michelangelo, in *Michelangelo: A Self-Portrait*.
30. Condivi, *The Life of Michelangelo*.
31. Hibbard, *Michelangelo*.
32. Quoted in Coughlan, *The World of Michelangelo*.
33. Georg Brandes, *Michelangelo: His Life, His Times, His Era*. Translated by Heinz Norden. New York: Frederick Ungar, 1963.
34. Vasari, *The Lives of the Painters, Sculptors, and Architects*.
35. Coughlan, *The World of Michelangelo*.
36. Michelangelo, in *Michelangelo: A Self-Portrait*.
37. Michelangelo, in *Michelangelo: A Self-Portrait*.
38. Michelangelo, in *Michelangelo: A Self-Portrait*.
39. Condivi, *The Life of Michelangelo*.
40. Coughlan, *The World of Michelangelo*.
41. Hibbard, *Michelangelo*.
42. da Vinci, *Treatise on Painting*.
43. Michelangelo, in *Michelangelo: A Self-*

Portrait.

44. Condivi, *The Life of Michelangelo.*

45. Vasari, *The Lives of the Painters, Sculptors, and Architects.*

46. Cellini, *The Autobiography.*

47. Vasari, *The Lives of the Painters, Sculptors, and Architects.*

48. Hibbard, *Michelangelo.*

49. Quoted in Hibbard, *Michelangelo.*

50. Brandes, *Michelangelo: His Life, His Times, His Era.*

51. Marcel Brion, *Michelangelo.* Translated by James Whitall. New York: Bonanza Books, 1940.

Chapter 5: The Sistine Chapel

52. Coughlan, *The World of Michelangelo.*

53. Brandes, *Michelangelo: His Life, His Times, His Era.*

54. Vasari, *The Lives of the Painters, Sculptors, and Architects.*

55. Michelangelo, in *Michelangelo: A Self-Portrait.*

56. Condivi, *The Life of Michelangelo.*

57. Vasari, *The Lives of the Painters, Sculptors, and Architects.*

58. Condivi, *The Life of Michelangelo.*

59. Quoted in Condivi, *The Life of Michelangelo.*

60. Michelangelo, in *Michelangelo: A Self-Portrait.*

61. Condivi, *The Life of Michelangelo.*

62. Brandes, *Michelangelo: His Life, His Times, His Era.*

63. Brion, *Michelangelo.*

64. Brandes, *Michelangelo: His Life, His Times, His Era.*

65. Vasari, *The Lives of the Painters, Sculptors, and Architects.*

66. Michelangelo, in *Michelangelo: A Self-Portrait.*

67. Michelangelo, in *Michelangelo: A Self-Portrait.*

68. Michelangelo, in *Michelangelo: A Self-Portrait.*

69. Vasari, *The Lives of the Painters, Sculptors, and Architects.*

70. Quoted in Brandes, *Michelangelo: His Life, His Times, His Era.*

71. Vasari, *The Lives of the Painters, Sculptors, and Architects.*

72. Brandes, *Michelangelo: His Life, His Times, His Era.*

73. Michelangelo, in *Michelangelo: A Self-Portrait.*

74. Michelangelo, in *Michelangelo: A Self-Portrait.*

75. Brandes, *Michelangelo: His Life, His Times, His Era.*

76. Hibbard, *Michelangelo.*

77. Michelangelo, in *Michelangelo: A Self-Portrait.*

Chapter 6: Breaking the Bonds and Chains of Tradition

78. Quoted in Brandes, *Michelangelo: His Life, His Times, His Era.*

79. Brion, *Michelangelo.*

80. Brandes, *Michelangelo: His Life, His Times, His Era.*

81. Hibbard, *Michelangelo.*

82. Quoted in Coughlan, *The World of Michelangelo.*

83. Condivi, *The Life of Michelangelo.*

84. Hibbard, *Michelangelo.*

85. Quoted in Coughlan, *The World of Michelangelo.*

86. Michelangelo, in *Michelangelo: A Self-Portrait.*

87. Brandes, *Michelangelo: His Life, His Times, His Era.*

88. de Tolnay, *Michelangelo.*

89. Quoted in Coughlan, *The World of Michelangelo.*

90. Condivi, *The Life of Michelangelo.*

91. Giovanni Mini, quoted in Brandes, *Michelangelo: His Life, His Times, His Era.*

92 Michelangelo, in *Michelangelo: A Self-Portrait.*

93. Condivi, *The Life of Michelangelo.*

94. Brandes, *Michelangelo: His Life, His Times, His Era.*

95. Hibbard, *Michelangelo.*

96. Vasari, *The Lives of the Painters, Sculptors, and Architects.*

97. Hibbard, *Michelangelo.*

98. Brandes, *Michelangelo: His Life, His Times, His Era.*

99. Vasari, *The Lives of the Painters, Sculptors, and Architects.*

Chapter 7: Friends and Religion

100. Brandes, *Michelangelo: His Life, His Times, His Era.*

101. Coughlan, *The World of Michelangelo.*

102. Hibbard, *Michelangelo.*

103. Michelangelo, in *Michelangelo: A Self-Portrait.*

104. Michelangelo, in *Michelangelo: A Self-Portrait.*

105. Michelangelo, in *Michelangelo: A Self-Portrait.*

106. Quoted in Condivi, *The Life of Michelangelo.*

107. Vittoria Colonna, quoted in Coughlan, *The World of Michelangelo.*

108. Sydney J. Freedberg, *Painting in Italy, 1500 to 1600.* Middlesex: Harmondsworth, 1979.

109. de Tolnay, *Michelangelo.*

110. Coughlan, *The World of Michelangelo.*

111. Coughlan, *The World of Michelangelo.*

112. Coughlan, *The World of Michelangelo.*

113. Michelangelo, in *Michelangelo: A Self-Portrait.*

114. Hibbard, *Michelangelo.*

115. Michelangelo, in *Michelangelo: A Self-Portrait.*

116. Hibbard, *Michelangelo.*

117. Vasari, *The Lives of the Painters, Sculptors, and Architects.*

118. Michelangelo, in *Michelangelo: A Self-Portrait.*

119. Quoted in Condivi, *The Life of Michelangelo.*

120. de Tolnay, *Michelangelo.*

121. Hibbard, *Michelangelo.*

122. de Tolnay, *Michelangelo.*

123. Michelangelo, in *Michelangelo: A Self-Portrait.*

Chapter 8: Michelangelo the Architect

124. Michelangelo, in *Michelangelo: A Self-Portrait.*

125. Quoted in Condivi, *The Life of Michelangelo.*

126. Michelangelo, in *Michelangelo: A Self-Portrait.*

127. Vasari, *The Lives of the Painters, Sculptors, and Architects.*

128. Quoted in Coughlan, *The World of Michelangelo.*

129. Vasari, *The Lives of the Painters, Sculptors, and Architects.*

130. Michelangelo, in *Michelangelo: A Self-Portrait.*

131. Michelangelo, in *Michelangelo: A Self-Portrait.*

132. Michelangelo, quoted in Coughlan, *The World of Michelangelo.*

133. Hibbard, *Michelangelo.*

134. de Tolnay, *Michelangelo.*

135. de Tolnay, *Michelangelo.*

136. Hibbard, *Michelangelo.*

137. John Addington Symonds, *The Life of Michelangelo Buonarroti.* New York: Random House Modern Library, 1936.

138. Hibbard, *Michelangelo.*

139. Quoted in Vasari, *The Lives of the Painters, Sculptors, and Architects.*

140. Quoted in Vasari, *The Lives of the Painters, Sculptors, and Architects.*

141. Quoted in Brandes, *Michelangelo: His Life, His Times, His Era.*

142. Michelangelo, quoted in Coughlan, *The World of Michelangelo.*

143. Vasari, *The Lives of the Painters, Sculptors, and Architects.*

Epilogue: A Towering Genius

144. Hibbard, *Michelangelo.*

For Further Reading

Ariane Ruskin Batterberry, *The Pantheon Story of Art*. New York: Pantheon Books, 1975.

Marshall B. Davidson, *A History of Art*. Random House Library of Knowledge series. New York: Random House, 1984.

Nathaniel Harris, *Leonardo and the Renaissance*. New York: The Bookwright Press, 1987.

Lutz Heusinger, *Michelangelo*. Library of Great Masters series. Lisa Clark Pilletti, tr. Florence, Italy: Scala/Riverside, 1990.

Christopher Hibbert, *The House of Medici: Its Rise and Fall*. New York: Morrow Quill Paperbacks, 1980.

H.W. Janson and Anthony F. Janson, *History of Art for Young People*. New York: Harry N. Abrams, 1992.

Richard McLanathan, *Leonardo da Vinci*. First Impressions series. New York: Harry N. Abrams, 1990.

Roberta M. Paine, *Looking at Architecture*. New York: Lothrop, Lee & Shepard, 1974.

Robin Richmond, *Introducing Michelangelo*. Boston: Little, Brown, 1992.

Irwin Shapiro, *The Golden Book of the Renaissance*. New York: Golden Books, 1962.

Piero Ventura, *Great Painters*. New York: G.P. Putnam's Sons, 1988.

Piero Ventura, *Michelangelo's World*. New York: G.P. Putnam's Sons, 1988.

Works Consulted

Bernard Berenson, *The Italian Painters of the Renaissance*. London: The Phaedon Press, 1967. A collection of essays written in 1896 and 1897 by the man still considered the foremost authority on the subject. Well-illustrated sections on each painter are fairly short, concentrating on styles rather than on biographical details.

Georg Brandes, *Michelangelo: His Life, His Times, His Era*. Heinz Norden, tr. New York: Frederick Ungar, 1963. Very readable biography with particularly good discussion of Italian politics and art prior to Michelangelo. Very few photographs and no index.

Marcel Brion, *Michelangelo*. James Whitall, tr. New York: Bonanza Books, 1940. A somewhat fanciful biography in which the author freely gives his own interpretation of Michelangelo's thoughts and motives. No photographs.

Jacob Burkhardt, *The Civilization of the Renaissance in Italy*. S.G.C. Middlemore, tr. New York: Harper & Row, 1958. A classic scholarly work on the Renaissance written in 1860 that proposed the general view, now disputed, that the Renaissance was a rebirth of ancient Greece and Rome and did not evolve at all from the Middle Ages.

Benvenuto Cellini, *The Autobiography*. John Addington Symonds, tr. New York: Grolier, 1978. Highly readable account of the adventures of this artist-soldier. Provides an excellent picture of life during the Renaissance.

Edward P. Cheyney, *The Dawn of a New Era*. New York: Harper & Row, 1936. First in the twenty-volume Rise of Modern Europe series. Gives very detailed accounts of the decline of the medieval church, the end of feudalism, and other movements leading up to the Renaissance.

Ascanio Condivi, *The Life of Michelangelo*. Alice Sedgwick Wohl, tr. Baton Rouge: Louisiana State University Press, 1976. A biography published in 1553, during Michelangelo's lifetime. Most of it was probably dictated to Condivi by Michelangelo, so it gives a good account of the way the artist viewed episodes in his life.

Robert Coughlan, *The World of Michelangelo: 1475-1564*. New York: Time-Life Books, 1966. Excellent overall account of the artist and his work. Especially helpful in describing how the political events of the time affected Michelangelo. There are plenty of good color photographs, including a foldout of the Sistine Chapel ceiling.

Karl H. Dannenfeldt, ed. *The Renaissance: Medieval or Modern?* Problems in European Civilization series. Ralph W. Greenlaw and Dwight E. Lee, eds. Lexington, MA: D.C. Heath, 1959. A collection of fourteen difficult essays on various subjects dealing with the Renaissance. Examines various interpretations of the reasons for and importance of the period.

Richard L. DeMolen, *Meaning of the Renaissance and Reformation*. New York: Houghton Mifflin, 1974. A collection of seven essays on the effects of the Renaissance in several European countries, with a good description of Renaissance Florence.

Charles de Tolnay, *Michelangelo*. Gaynor Woodhouse, tr. Princeton, NJ: Princeton University Press, 1975. Originally published in the 1940s, this five-volume series remains the most comprehensive and authoritative work on Michelangelo. More attention is given to discussion of the artist's works than details of his life. Contains photographs of every work by Michelangelo.

Wallace K. Ferguson, *The Renaissance*. New York: Holt, Rinehart & Winston, 1940.

Short, readable, and well-organized account of the transition from the Middle Ages to the Renaissance. Very clear account of how the decline of the church and the nobility and the rise of a merchant class led to new ways of thinking.

Sydney J. Freedberg, *Painting in Italy: 1500 to 1600.* Middlesex, England: Harmondworth, 1979. Part of the *Penguin History of Art* series. Gives detailed descriptions of the evolution of painting in various sections of Italy during each part of the century. Good, readable text; many photographs but none, unfortunately, in color.

Sydney J. Freedberg, *Painting of the Renaissance in Rome and Florence.* Cambridge, MA: Harvard University Press, 1961. Includes comprehensive discussions of the painting of Leonardo da Vinci, Raphael, and Michelangelo. Especially good sections on the Sistine Chapel ceiling and on links between ancient art and the Renaissance.

John R. Hale, *Renaissance.* New York: Time-Life Books, 1965. Very good overall introduction to the Renaissance. Chapters on art and on Florence are especially valuable in the study of Michelangelo. Very good pictures throughout.

George Heard Hamilton, *19th and 20th Century Art.* Englewood Cliffs, NJ: Prentice-Hall, 1975. Comprehensive account of developments in art and architecture from Romantic classicism to surrealism. There are many pictures, but few are in color.

Julius S. Held and Donald Posner, *17th and 18th Century Art.* Englewood Cliffs, NJ: Prentice-Hall, 1979. Very detailed description of how art developed in each country of Europe during the time period covered. American, Asian, and African art are ignored. Few color pictures.

Howard Hibbard, *Michelangelo.* 2d ed. New York: Harper & Row, 1974. Good, modern biography that follows Michelangelo's career chronologically by works. Uses quotations from Vasari, Condivi, and Michelangelo to illustrate points.

Elizabeth Elias Kaufman, *Michelangelo.* Secaucus, NJ: Castle Books, 1980. Very good color pictures of some of Michelangelo's major works, but very little text.

Leonardo da Vinci, *Treatise on Painting.* A. Philip McMahon, tr. Princeton, NJ: Princeton University Press, 1956. Leonardo's views on the art of painting and sculpture.

Michelangelo Buonarroti, *Michelangelo: A Self-Portrait.* Robert J. Clements, ed. New York: New York University Press, 1968. A collection of the most revealing of Michelangelo's many letters, poems, and sayings arranged by topic. Gives an excellent view of the artist through his own words.

Bernard S. Myers, ed., *Encyclopedia of Painting.* 4th ed. New York: Crown, 1979. Good, basic reference book on the subject of painting. Well-illustrated, short articles on artists, movements, and techniques. Very good explanations of technical terms.

John Addington Symonds, *The Life of Michelangelo Buonarroti.* New York: Random House Modern Library, 1936. First published in 1893, this is one of the most complete yet readable biographies of Michelangelo. A must for anyone studying the artist. Lack of index is a drawback.

Giorgio Vasari, *The Lives of the Painters, Sculptors, and Architects.* A.B. Hinds, tr. London: J.M. Dent & Sons, 1973. Short biographies of all major and minor figures of Italian Renaissance art. The section on Michelangelo is the best primary source for biographical details. The chatty style is easy to follow, except when the author becomes bogged down in lengthy descriptions of some works.

Martin Weinberger, *Michelangelo the Sculptor.* London: Routledge & Kegan Paul, 1967. Comprehensive but highly technical account of Michelangelo's sculpture. The text is in one volume and the photographs are in another, which is awkward.

Index

Picture Credits

Cover Photo: Historical Pictures/Stock Montage

Alinari/Art Resource, New York, 25, 33 (top), 40, 51, 55, 60 (right), 63, 67 (top), 75, 85, 86

The Bettmann Archive, 8, 30, 35, 37, 42, 48, 57, 58 (both), 59, 60 (left), 73 (top), 74, 77 (both), 80, 83, 84, 89, 91, 93

Bridgeman/Art Resource, New York, 44

Historical Pictures/Stock Montage, 9, 16, 23 (right), 26, 49, 53 (top), 64, 71, 72, 87

The Metropolitan Museum of Art, Harris Brisbane Dick Fund, 1941, (41.72), 92 (bottom)

North Wind Picture Archives, 14 (both), 19, 20, 21, 23 (left), 24, 27, 31, 33 (bottom), 41, 53 (bottom), 62, 65, 67 (bottom), 69, 70, 92 (top), 96

Scala/Art Resource, New York, 95, 98

SEF/Art Resource, New York, 90

UPI/Bettmann, 78, 79, 99

Acknowledgments

The following publishers have generously given permission to use extended quotations from copyrighted works: From *The Lives of the Painters, Sculptors, and Architects* by Giorgio Vasari, translated by A.B. Hinds. Reproduced, with permission, from the Everyman's Library edition, © 1973 by David Campbell Publishers, Ltd. From *Michelangelo: A Self-Portrait*, edited by Robert J. Clements. New York: New York University Press, 1968. Reprinted with permission. From *Time-Life Library of Art: The World of Michelangelo* by Robert Coughlan and the editors of Time-Life Books © 1966 Time-Life Books Inc. Reprinted with permission. From *The Life of Michelangelo* by Ascansio Condivi. Translated by Alice Sedgwick Wohl, edited by Hellmut Wohl. Copyright © 1976 by Alice Sedgwick Wohl and Hellmut Wohl. Reprinted by permission of Louisiana State University Press.

About the Author

William W. Lace is a native of Fort Worth, Texas. He holds a bachelor's degree from Texas Christian University, a master's from East Texas State University, and a doctorate from the University of North Texas. After working for newspapers in Baytown, Texas, and Fort Worth, he joined the University of Texas at Arlington as sports information director and later became the director of the news service. He is now director of college relations for the Tarrant County Junior College District in Fort Worth. He and his wife, Laura, live in Arlington and have two children. Lace has written one other book, a biography of baseball player Nolan Ryan.